D0129535

B

# Favorite Quilts from Anka's Treasures

## Heather Mulder Peterson

*Martingale*®
& COMPANY

Favorite Quilts from Anka's Treasures
© 2007 by Heather Mulder Peterson

That Patchwork Place® is an imprint of Martingale & Company®.

Martingale & Company
20205 144th Ave. NE
Woodinville, WA 98072-8478
www.martingale-pub.com

No part of this product may be reproduced in any form, unless otherwise stated, in which case reproduction is limited to the use of the purchaser. The written instructions, photographs, designs, projects, and patterns are intended for the personal, noncommercial use of the retail purchaser and are under federal copyright laws; they are not to be reproduced by any electronic, mechanical, or other means, including informational storage or retrieval systems, for commercial use. Permission is granted to photocopy patterns for the personal use of the retail purchaser.

The information in this book is presented in good faith, but no warranty is given nor results guaranteed. Since Martingale & Company has no control over choice of materials or procedures, the company assumes no responsibility for the use of this information.

Printed in China
12 11 10 09 08 07        8 7 6 5 4 3 2

**Library of Congress Cataloging-in-Publication Data**
Library of Congress Control Number: 2006026559
ISBN: 978-1-56477-714-0

## MISSION STATEMENT

Dedicated to providing quality products and service to inspire creativity.

## CREDITS

President — Nancy J. Martin
CEO — Daniel J. Martin
COO — Tom Wierzbicki
Publisher — Jane Hamada
Editorial Director — Mary V. Green
Managing Editor — Tina Cook
Technical Editor — Laurie Bevan
Copy Editor — Melissa Bryan
Design Director — Stan Green
Illustrator — Laurel Strand
Cover and Text Designer — Shelly Garrison
Photographer — Brent Kane

## DEDICATION

To all of you who have supported my business. You have made it possible for me to do what I love and have given me such an enjoyable past 10 years. Thank you!

## ACKNOWLEDGMENTS

I want to give a special thanks to my two biggest supporters—my mom, Deb, and my husband, Joel. My mom has put in an unbelievable amount of hours helping me, sustained by diet cola, chocolate, and good movies. She is always willing to play the sounding board, and helps to ease my burden when it's crunch time. I have so many great memories of working and playing together. I can never thank her enough for all she does and for teaching me to sew in the first place.

Joel, thank you for all your encouragement, love, and support in life and in my quilting endeavors. Also, thanks for being a willing travel partner—although you always seem to manage to squeeze in a fishing trip wherever we're traveling for my teaching jobs! I appreciate your positive attitude and your ever-willing visits to quilt shops simply to pick up fabric or drop off quilts.

# Contents

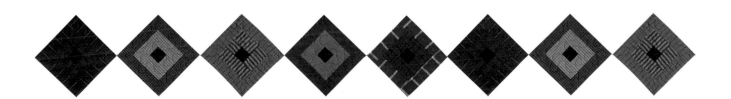

# Introduction

My business, Anka's Treasures, was named after a very inspirational person to me—my great-grandma Anka Petersen. She began the family tradition of sewing by teaching my mom how to sew, and then my mom passed that gift on to me.

Like many of you, I became aware of quilting at an early age. But those quilts were mostly utilitarian items that a grandma or great-aunt had made. You know the type—tied, with lots of polyester fabric. I remember, years ago, how I would use a cardboard template to cut squares from a drapery sample book, and then sew the squares together to make a quilt for my playhouse. At the time, that was all I knew of quilting, and it wasn't until years later that a new kind of quilting began to reveal itself to me. It started when a friend of my mom's convinced her to take a class at the local quilt shop. I was observing the fun Mom was having with her new hobby. She was making a sampler quilt, so I started hearing terms like strip piecing, shoo-fly, churn dash, and flying geese. That winter I had a week off from school for Christmas break and I decided to try my hand at quilting. I started with one of the sampler blocks. As soon as one was finished, I started another. By the end of the week I had the entire sampler quilt done (almost 20 blocks). Needless to say, I was immediately addicted. I remember my first trip to a quilt shop to buy fabric—and thus began another addiction. Obviously I had no idea what I was getting myself into.

Since then quilting has played a huge part in my life. It's not just my hobby, it's my job. It has been a great source of joy and inspiration. Through a collection of my favorite designs, I hope to bring the same to the readers of this book. I look forward to sharing my ideas on appliqué with you, as well as my piecing techniques. I want to encourage quilters to expand their abilities by learning how simple appliqué techniques, color coordination, and basic piecing can produce eye-catching results. I still remember being a beginner, so I try to make the process as easy as possible, without compromising the design. My designing and tastes have changed over the years, but I have tried to include a little something for everyone. I have even included some color options to help you envision the endless possibilities.

I have been dreaming of this book for several years now. One of my business goals has been to write a 10-year anniversary book showcasing my favorite designs. This book is the result of that dream. Choosing the quilts has been a hard task but has given me a chance to revisit my favorite designs and reminisce about days gone by. I'm not the type of designer who begins with a grand vision of a quilt in my head, with all things flowing smoothly from start to finish. Many times it's a brain-racking process during which things just don't work out—ask to see my reject pile! That's why I want to celebrate the quilts that did come together, the ones that have inspired other quilters. I have chosen designs that have struck chords with my customers and also contain many key elements of my approach to quilting. Through these designs, I wish to share with you, the readers, much of the same sense of fulfillment that I gain from quilting. I hope the quilts that fill these pages will soon be filling your own rooms. I know they have brought me much joy, not only through the process of making them, but also through the comfort and beauty they provide as they surround me in my home.

# General Instructions

Everyone needs a little help now and then, and this is the section to turn to when you do.

## Selecting and Preparing Fabrics

Selecting colors is such a fun part of quilting. I have several hints to share that may help you in your color selection. I often start with a feature fabric such as a large floral that has many colors to pull from. I then use this feature fabric to inspire the color selection for my quilt. If you like all the colors together in the feature fabric, chances are you'll be happy with how they work together in the quilt, too. I'm often inspired by fabric lines as well. The designers and fabric companies have gone to a lot of effort to coordinate the colors and prints so they work well together. I choose my favorite prints from the line and make the entire quilt with those fabrics. This eliminates all the guesswork involved in color coordinating. Many shops now display these collections together so that you can easily select your fabrics.

Whether I'm designing a fabric line or picking fabrics for a quilt, I include a variety of prints—small-, medium-, and large-scale prints, along with some geometrics, florals, tonals, and even plaids and stripes. Having a variety will add interest. You will also want to consider the size of your quilt when picking the scale of your fabrics. Large-scale prints don't usually work well in a quilt with small pieces, but they look wonderful in a quilt with large pieces. Also, I always include what I call "connector" fabrics. A connector fabric draws everything together by including bits of several colors that reappear throughout the quilt.

I love to include black in my color selection. Black may not seem like a color you would normally consider, but I love what it does for the other colors in the quilt. Adding black to the color scheme grounds an otherwise busy quilt and makes all the colors sparkle. I think my love of black kept me from using pastels and lighter colors for years; it just didn't come naturally for me. But look at some of the quilts in this book and you can see that now I'm branching out and using a bigger variety of colors.

Choose only 100%-cotton fabrics of the highest quality you can afford. Cotton is wonderful to work with, is durable, and has "memory" when you are pressing. If desired, wash and press all your fabrics before beginning. If you don't plan to wash your fabrics, be sure to test any fabrics that are questionable and may bleed or shrink.

## Tools

Quilters today are living in a great time with an abundance of tools that make quilting easier. In fact, there are so many that it becomes overwhelming to pick and choose. To simplify things, I'm just listing a few basic necessities.

**Sewing machine.** You will need a reliable machine, with proper tension that sews a good straight stitch. If you are going to do your appliqué by machine like I do, you will also need zigzag-stitch and blanket-stitch features. A ¼" foot is a wonderful machine accessory to have and will greatly improve your accuracy. An open-toe foot for appliqué is another favorite accessory of mine.

**Thread.** I use a cotton-covered polyester thread for all my piecing and machine quilting. Also good, but not quite as strong, is 100%-cotton thread. Be sure to have several neutral colors on hand in light, medium, and dark.

**Measuring and cutting tools.** You will want to purchase a rotary cutter, self-healing mat, and acrylic rulers. These will become some of your most frequently used quilting tools. Be sure that your acrylic rulers have ⅛" markings. You will want to start with 6" x 12" and 6" x 24" rulers, adding other sizes as needed. An 18" x 24" mat will accommodate all the cutting for the projects in this book, but, again, you could eventually obtain a couple of different sizes.

**Pins.** Most quilters develop a preference for a certain type of pin. I prefer the extra-long quilter's pins with plastic or glass heads. These pins are very thin and sharp, allowing them to glide through fabrics easily.

**Needles.** You will need a variety of needles for quilting, for both machine sewing and handwork. I do my piecing with an 80/12 needle, but I use several sizes for appliqué. (See "Appliqué" on page 9 for more information.) For doing handwork such as appliqué or turning binding, I use straw needles.

**Iron and ironing board.** It's best to find a lightweight iron with a nonstick surface. I also like an iron with good steam.

**Additional tools.** Paper scissors and a fine-tip marking pen or pencil will always come in handy.

## Rotary Cutting

I cut all my strips crosswise rather than lengthwise, because shorter crosswise strips are easier both to cut and to sew.

1. Fold the fabric in half, lining up the selvages. Lay the fabric on a mat, with the fold nearest you, being sure there are no twists along the fold. To square up the raw edge of the fabric, align a square ruler with the folded edge, and then butt a long ruler's right-hand edge against the square ruler as shown.

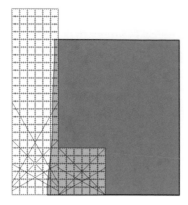

2. Set the square ruler aside and then cut along the edge of the long ruler. Always cut away from you, not toward your body.

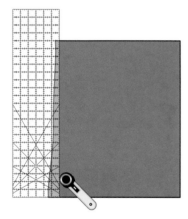

3. Begin cutting strips from the straight edge of the fabric. If you're cutting multiple strips from one piece of fabric, periodically stop and square up your fabric edge again before continuing.

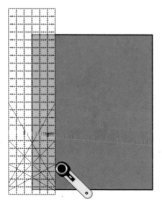

4. To cut a strip into smaller sections, turn it and square up the end, as you did with the large piece of fabric. Cut pieces from this straight edge, making your way across the strip until you have the number of pieces required. Once you're comfortable with rotary cutting, you can layer a couple of strips on top of one another and cut several layers at once. This will greatly reduce the amount of time you spend cutting.

## Piecing

Before you begin sewing, you need to make sure that you are using an exact ¼" seam allowance. The best way to achieve an accurate seam allowance is with a special foot measuring ¼" from the center needle position to the edge of the foot. You may also mark your machine with masking tape and use that as a guide. If you are unsure what your seam allowance is, you can sew three 1½" x 5" strips together lengthwise. Press, and then measure the middle strip. If the strip isn't exactly 1", you know your seam allowance is off. Even a thread or two matters and can result in blocks, sashing, or borders that don't fit together.

When joining pieces, lay them right sides together unless otherwise stated. To help save time and thread, you will want to chain piece. This means you sew directly from one piece to the next, without stopping and snipping the threads. After all the pieces are sewn, then you can clip the threads in between.

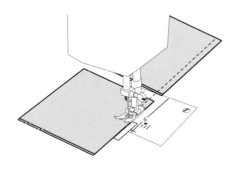

### STRIP-PIECED UNITS

Rather than sewing individual pieces together, you will often be directed to cut strips, sew them together, and then cut the strip sets into smaller segments. When cutting the segments, align the markings on your ruler with the seam lines on your strip sets to ensure that your pieces stay square.

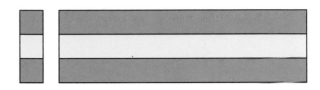

### FOLDED-CORNER UNITS

Draw a diagonal line from corner to corner on the wrong side of a square or strip. Lay the piece right sides together with a larger square or rectangle and sew on the drawn line. Cut off the outside corner, leaving a ¼" seam allowance, and press as directed.

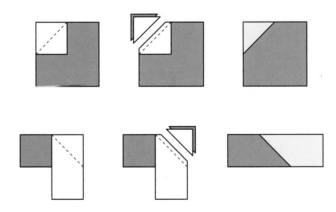

### HALF-SQUARE-TRIANGLE UNITS

Lay two squares right sides together and draw a diagonal line across the wrong side of the top square. Sew ¼" from both sides of the line and cut on the drawn line. Press the seams as directed. This will yield two half-square-triangle units.

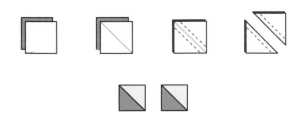

## QUARTER-SQUARE-TRIANGLE UNITS

Lay two half-square-triangle units right sides together with different fabrics facing each other. Draw a diagonal line across the wrong side of the top unit as shown. Sew ¼" from both sides of the line and cut on the drawn line. Press the seams as directed.

## PINNING AND NESTING

I prefer to spend as little time as possible pinning—I'd rather be sewing! But to make this possible, I must plan my pressing so that my seam allowances will go in opposite directions when they come together. This helps the pieces "nest" nicely. I do use pins, however, on complicated intersections that need to be matched, or when I'm sewing on my borders.

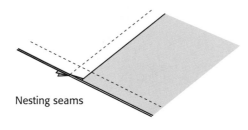

Nesting seams

## PRESSING

It's important to press seams as you go. In this book, pressing instructions or arrows are generally given in the project instructions. If they aren't, press the seams toward the darker fabric or in the direction that creates the least amount of bulk. It's also OK to press the seams open. I like to use a steam iron so that my seams lie nice and flat. Just be careful not to stretch or misshape your pieces when you are pressing.

## PROOFING

As you work on the projects in this book, many of the steps will instruct you to "proof" a block or section to a certain size. This means laying a ruler on top of the unit to verify that its measurements are correct. If they're not, you will need to make any necessary adjustments before going on.

## ADDING THE BORDERS

The border measurements in this book reflect the actual mathematical measures. Due to variations in workmanship, they will not be the same for each quilter. Measure your own quilt as you go and then cut the border pieces to that length. I usually measure in three places (at each edge and across the middle) and then take an average. I mark the middle of the border strips and line this up with the middle of the quilt top. I add a few extra pins, and as I'm sewing I make sure that the border works in and fits the quilt. I sew the borders to the sides of the quilt first, and then to the top and bottom.

# Appliqué

Be open to the possibilities that appliqué can offer. I love it because it has allowed me to go further into my favorite craft—quilting. Many shapes are virtually impossible to piece, and, surprisingly, some shapes are actually faster to create and more realistic looking with appliqué. I also think that adding appliqué to your quilt top offers unlimited possibilities for originality.

I'm on a limited time schedule and there are many quilts I want to make, so I use what I have found to be the fastest, most user-friendly appliqué method. Other methods can be substituted, but if you would like to try the fusible-machine method that I used for the projects in this book, refer to the following instructions.

## Preparing the Shapes

I have several things that I consider when I appliqué and they all work together to produce good results. I try to use the simplest shapes possible without compromising the design. For example, that means using a simple outline of a flower, rather than attempting to create multiple petals, flower centers, and so on. Also, I don't add large quantities of pieces that aren't needed. For example, my vines may have only 5 leaves, instead of 20. Sometimes these details are enough to make appliqué faster and easier for quilters.

Start by buying a lightweight fusible product. Read through and follow the manufacturer's instructions. Trace the appliqué pattern onto the paper side of the fusible material. (All patterns in this book have already been reversed.) Leave ¼" to ½" between the shapes and roughly cut them out around the drawn lines. On the larger or layered shapes, I find it very important to trim out the center of the fusible material, leaving roughly ¼"

of glue around the edges. This helps to reduce bulk and stiffness. Iron the shapes to the wrong side of the fabric and cut them out on the drawn line. Peel off the paper backing and fuse to the right side of the project.

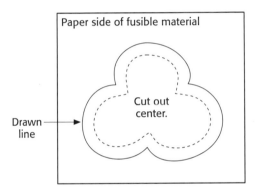

## Setting Up the Machine

Achieving a successful appliqué experience depends on using the right tools and materials, such as threads, sewing-machine feet, and needles. For blanket-stitching I prefer a heavy thread called top-stitching thread. It gives the look of hand blanket-stitching and is machine friendly. For a small zigzag stitch, I use a regular-weight thread that matches the color of the appliqué piece.

If you're going to machine appliqué, an open-toe foot is essential. It allows you to see where you're going, with enough time to react around sharp curves. A clear foot is another alternative but isn't quite as helpful.

The right type of needle can also make the difference between a fun experience and a frustrating session filled with skipped stitches and fraying and breaking threads. Consult the following chart when determining needle size.

|  | Zigzag Stitch | Blanket Stitch |
|---|---|---|
| **When to Use** | For small, curved, or detailed shapes | For large shapes and gentle curves, or for a decorative look |
| **Type of Thread** | Regular weight, matching color | Topstitching-weight thread; two strands of regular thread will also work. This can be done in an accent color or a matching color. |
| **Bobbin** | Regular weight | Regular weight |
| **Needle Size** | #9 or #10 to reduce fraying the edges of the appliqué shape | #12 to #18. If you are having trouble with skipped stitches or breaking thread, try a larger needle. |
| **Stitch Width** | 1/16" | 3/16" |
| **Stitch Length** | 1/32" | 3/16" |
| **Presser Foot** | I use an open-toe foot for appliquéing. ||
| **Tension** | I always loosen the top tension a tiny bit—just so the thread "dots" appear on the back of the block and not the front. ||
| **Options** | Many machines have different options to help make the process easier, such as the needle-down button, mirror-image function, half-speed stitching, and double blanket stitch, to name a few. Explore your machine to see if you have any of these helpful features. ||
| **Securing** | To secure your stitching, you can do several stitches in place and then trim the ends. If you are using heavy topstitching thread, leave tails when starting and stopping and pull them to the back of the block. Tie a double knot and then trim. ||

## Appliquéing the Shapes

I use a combination of two basic stitches: the blanket stitch and a small zigzag stitch. I use the blanket stitch on large decorative shapes and the small zigzag on the delicate, curvy, or detailed shapes for which the blanket stitch isn't as easy to maneuver. I often use both stitches on one appliqué design, choosing the zigzag stitch on smaller shapes such as flower centers, stems, and leaves, and opting for the blanket stitch on the remaining larger shapes. Carefully analyze the shapes before you start appliquéing, deciding how and where to add each piece.

Blanket stitch                    Small zigzag stitch

Particularly for beginners, I want to encourage you to choose appliqué shapes carefully, starting with the large, simple shapes (see "Rickrack Roses" on page 45). Don't start out doing a miniature moose appliqué. Trying to pivot around all those skinny antlers will probably result in that appliqué being your last.

There is a learning curve that goes with machine appliqué. Like so many other things, it takes practice. You shouldn't expect to be perfect on your first try. On the first day of basketball practice, you can't expect to dribble between your legs and behind your back. Appliquéing is much the same way, and you have to be a bit determined to get through the initial clumsy feelings. But once you've got it, the possibilities are endless.

Now that your machine is set up and you have chosen and prepared your appliqué shapes, you are ready to give machine appliqué a try. To begin, align your stitches as shown, keeping the stitching almost entirely on the appliqué shape and going just over the edge into the ditch where the appliqué and the background meet. The goal is to just barely cover the edge of the fabric; the bulk of the stitching should be on top of the shape.

Correct       Incorrect

## APPLIQUÉING INSIDE POINTS

When appliquéing inside points, you'll take a different approach depending on whether you're using a zigzag or a blanket stitch.

For the zigzag stitch, begin stitching a short distance away from an inside point as shown and stitch up to the pivot point. Pivot and continue stitching. A gap in your stitching indicates an error in pivot position.

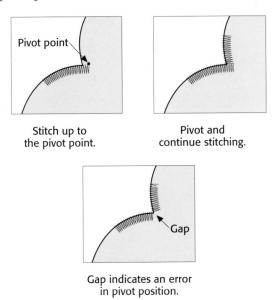

Pivot point

Stitch up to the pivot point.

Pivot and continue stitching.

Gap

Gap indicates an error in pivot position.

For the blanket stitch, begin stitching a short distance away from an inside point as shown and stitch up to the stopping point. Pivot and take one stitch. Pivot again and continue stitching.

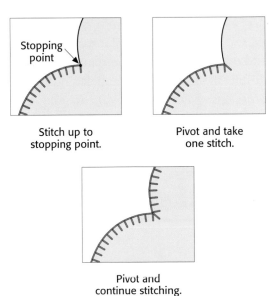

Stopping point

Stitch up to stopping point.

Pivot and take one stitch.

Pivot and continue stitching.

## APPLIQUÉING OUTSIDE POINTS

When appliquéing outside points, you'll again take a different approach depending on whether you're using a zigzag or a blanket stitch.

For the zigzag stitch, begin stitching a short distance away from an outside point as shown and stitch up to the pivot point. Pivot and continue stitching.

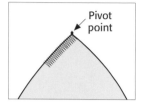
Stitch up to the pivot point.

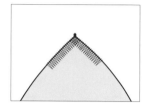
Pivot and continue stitching.

For the blanket stitch, begin stitching a short distance away from an outside point as shown and stitch up to the stopping point. Pivot and take one stitch. Pivot again and continue stitching.

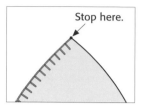
Stitch up to stopping point.

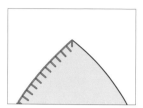
Pivot and take one stitch.

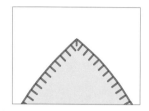
Pivot and continue stitching.

# Finishing

Once your quilt top is complete, only a few final steps remain. The quilting process allows an additional opportunity for design creativity, while the addition of the binding gives the quilt a polished appearance. And don't forget to add a hanging sleeve so that you can display your project for others to enjoy.

## Quilting

All the projects in this book are quilted by machine, but you can use any quilting method you prefer. To begin, make sure that your backing and batting are at least 4" wider and longer than the quilt top. Layer the batting between the backing and the quilt top, and quilt as desired. Because I'm a machine quilter, I create many of my designs freehand; but if I have to mark, I do it as I go with a stencil and a chalk pouncer. A chalk pouncer is a little fabric bag filled with powdered chalk that you tap along the stencil to transfer the pattern to the quilt top.

## Hanging Sleeve

To make a hanging sleeve for displaying your quilt, cut a fabric strip 5" wide and the length of the top side of the quilt. Fold both short ends under and hem about ¾". Press in half with wrong sides together so the strip is 2½" wide. Sew to the back of the quilt, lining up the raw edge of the sleeve with the raw edge of the quilt back. The raw edge will be hidden after you have hand stitched the binding down.

## Binding

The patterns in this book include yardage for binding that is cut 2½" wide. Be sure to allow for more fabric if you would like to cut yours wider. I use the traditional French double-fold method.

1. Overlap the ends of the binding strips right sides together as shown. Sew diagonally from corner to corner; trim off the outside corner, and press.

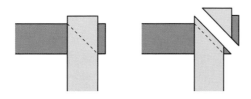

2. Press the strip in half with wrong sides together. Leaving an 8" tail, start sewing the binding to the quilt top with a scant ⅜" seam allowance. Miter the corners as shown.

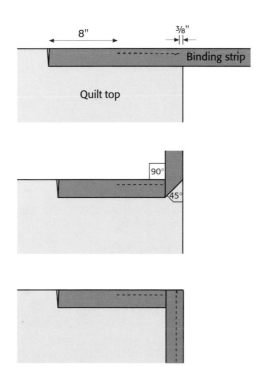

3. Stop sewing when you are about 13" from the beginning point. There are many methods for finishing the binding, several of which result in a bulky end. I prefer a continuous binding, without a visible ending point. The trick is knowing how long to cut your tails. Start by laying out the beginning tail as shown and then overlap the ending tail. The length of the overlap needs to be the same as the width of the binding. For example, if you're using a 2½"-wide binding, the strips need to overlap by 2½". (You can even use a scrap of your binding as your "template.") Sew the two ends together as shown and trim, leaving a ¼" seam allowance. Press the seam, reposition the binding on the quilt, and finish sewing. Nobody will be able to tell where you ended, and there is no math and no complicated angles!

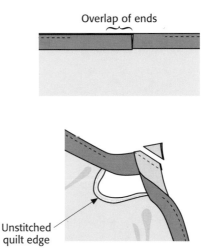

4. Fold the edge of the binding to the back of the quilt and hand stitch down, mitering the corners. I use one strand of hand-quilting thread for this step.

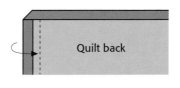

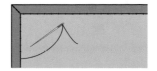

# Sweet Dreams

Ɩn this simple quilt, two easy blocks are combined to produce a secondary design—a Four Patch block. I love little surprises like that. There is no appliqué on this quilt, making it easy enough for even a beginner to tackle. The optional scalloped border adds a bit of extra charm.

## Materials

*Yardage is based on 42"-wide fabric.*

12 fat quarters in assorted colors for blocks

2½ yards of yellow plaid for blocks and outer border

1¾ yards of cream fabric for blocks and setting triangles

1⅓ yards of blue dot fabric for inner border and binding

5 yards of fabric for backing

76" x 90" piece of batting

## Cutting

**From the assorted fat quarters, cut:**
20 sets* of:

    1 square, 6½" x 6½"

    4 squares, 2¼" x 2¼"

20 sets of 4 pieces, 2¼" x 6½"*

12 sets of 4 squares, 2¼" x 2¼"*

14 squares, 2¼" x 2¼"

*Cut each set from 1 fabric for a consistent look within each block.*

**From the cream fabric, cut:**
5 strips, 3⅞" x 42"; crosscut into 48 squares, 3⅞" x 3⅞". Cut each square once diagonally to yield 96 triangles.

4 squares, 12¼" x 12¼"; cut each square twice diagonally to yield 16 side triangles. (You will use 14.)

2 squares, 7⅝" x 7⅝"; cut each square once diagonally to yield 4 corner triangles

4 strips, 2¼" x 42"; crosscut into 14 pieces, 2¼" x 9"

**From the yellow plaid, cut:**
11 strips, 7¼" x 42"; crosscut *3 strips* into 12 squares, 7¼" x 7¼"

**From the blue dot fabric, cut:**
7 strips, 2¼" x 42"

2½"-wide bias strips to total 350" in length

## Making the Blocks

1. Lay out the 20 sets of matching 6½" and 2¼" colored squares along with the 20 sets of 2¼" x 6½" colored pieces, arranging them in pleasing color combinations. Sew each block together as shown, pressing the seams as directed by the arrows. Proof each block to 10" x 10".

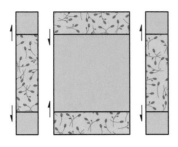

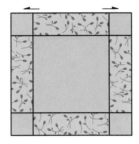

Make 20.

2. Using the 3⅞" cream triangles and the 12 sets of 2¼" colored squares, sew a triangle to each square as shown. Press toward the cream and trim off one triangle point as shown. Sew another cream triangle to the unit and press the seam as directed.

Make 48.

Quilt size: 71¼" x 84¾"

3. Sew four matching units from step 2 to a yellow plaid square as shown and press the seams as directed by the arrows. Make 12 of these blocks and proof each block to 10" x 10".

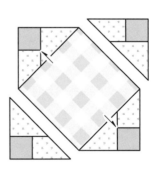

Make 12.

4. Sew one of the remaining 2¼" colored squares to an end of each 2¼" x 9" cream piece. Press toward the cream. Sew a large cream triangle to each unit as shown. Press as directed by the arrow and trim the end of each 9" cream piece to align with the triangle. Make 14.

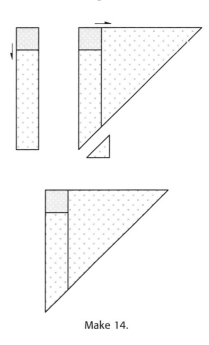

Make 14.

## Assembling the Quilt Top

1. Lay out the 20 colored blocks, the 12 plaid blocks, and the side and corner triangles as shown. Sew the blocks into rows and press the seams toward the colored blocks. Sew the rows together and press the seams in either direction. Add the corner triangles last and press the seams toward the corners. Proof the quilt center to 54¼" x 67¾".

2. Referring to "Adding the Borders" on page 8 as needed, sew all the blue dot strips together end to end. Cut off two lengths at 67¾" and sew them to the sides of the quilt-top center. Cut off two lengths at 57¾" and sew these to the top and bottom of the quilt top. Press all the seams toward the blue dot border.

3. Sew the yellow plaid strips together in pairs end to end to make four long strips. Cut each strip to a length of 71¼". Sew two of these

border strips to the sides of the quilt top, and then sew the remaining border strips to the top and bottom. Press all the seams toward the blue dot border.

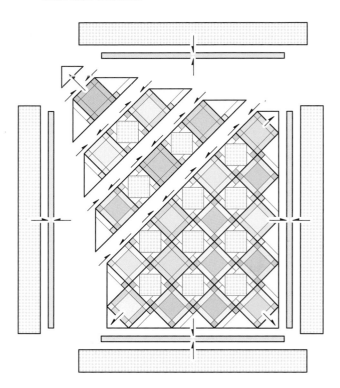

## Finishing

Refer to the quilt-finishing techniques on pages 12–13, if needed.

1. Piece the quilt backing so that it's approximately 4" wider and longer than the quilt top. Mark the quilt top if necessary. If you choose to scallop your border, the scallop patterns are on page 18. Mark the scallop designs on the borders before quilting, and trim along the lines after quilting. Layer the quilt top with batting and backing, and baste the layers together. Hand or machine quilt as desired.

2. Trim the batting and backing even with the edges of the quilt top. Add a hanging sleeve if desired. Using the 2½"-wide blue dot bias strips, prepare the binding and sew it to the quilt.

## COLOR OPTION

I chose a pack of fat quarters to make this quilt variation. It's so easy, as all the work of color coordinating has already been done for you by the fabric company.

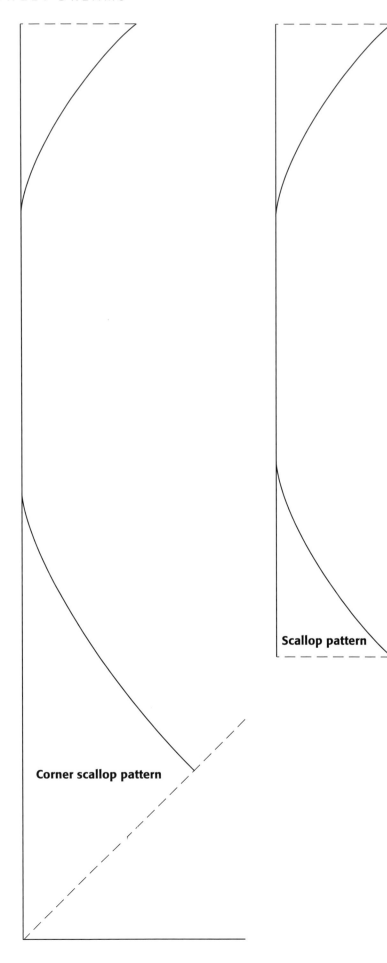

**Scallop pattern**

**Corner scallop pattern**

# On a Whim

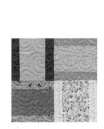

$I$f you are on a tight time schedule, this is the quilt for you. It goes together quickly and is easy enough for a beginner. As a bonus, it looks good in many different color combinations, so let the fabric do the work and save yourself time by avoiding intricate piecing.

## Materials

*Yardage is based on 42"-wide fabric.*

11 fat quarters *or* 2¾ yards *total* of assorted colors for blocks

⅞ yard of yellow print for outer border

½ yard of dark pink fabric for inner border

⅝ yard of blue plaid for binding

3½ yards of fabric for backing

58" x 72" piece of batting

## Cutting

**From the assorted colors, cut:**
48 pairs* of 2 strips, 1⅞" x 7½" (96 total)
48 rectangles, 4¾" x 7½"
4 squares, 1⅞" x 1⅞" (inner border posts)

**From the dark pink fabric, cut:**
6 strips, 1⅞" x 42"

**From the yellow print, cut:**
6 strips, 4½" x 42"

**From the blue plaid, cut:**
2½"-wide bias strips to total 250" in length

*Cut each pair from 1 fabric for a consistent look within each block.*

## Making the Blocks

Sew pairs of colored strips to the long edges of colored rectangles in pleasing color combinations. Press the seams toward the strips. Proof each block to 7½" x 7½".

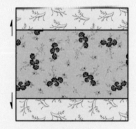

**Make 48.**

## Assembling the Quilt Top

1. Sew the blocks into eight rows of six blocks each. Press the seams as directed by the arrows. Sew the rows together and press the seams in either direction. Proof the quilt top to 42½" x 56½".

2. Referring to "Adding the Borders" on page 8 as needed, sew the dark pink strips together end to end. Cut off two lengths at 56½", two lengths at 42½", and eight pieces at 4½". Sew the yellow print strips together end to end. Cut

Quilt size: 53¼" x 67¼"

off two lengths at 56½", two lengths at 42½", and four squares, 4½" x 4½".

3. Sew a 1⅞" colored square, two 4½" dark pink pieces, and one yellow square together as shown.

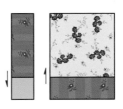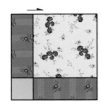

Make 4.

4. Sew the matching lengths of dark pink and yellow strips together in pairs; press toward the dark pink. Sew the 56½"-long strip pairs to the sides of the quilt top center and press the seams toward the dark pink. Sew the corner units from step 3 to the ends of the 42½"-long strip pairs as shown, pressing the seams toward the strip pairs. Sew these border strips to the top and bottom of the quilt top and press the seams as directed.

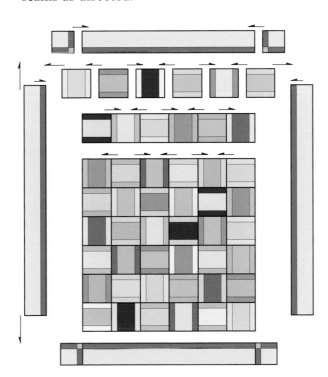

## Finishing

Refer to the quilt-finishing techniques on pages 12–13, if needed.

1. Piece the quilt backing so that it's approximately 4" wider and longer than the quilt top. Mark the quilt top if necessary. Layer the quilt top with batting and backing, and baste the layers together. Hand or machine quilt as desired.

2. Trim the batting and backing even with the edges of the quilt top. Add a hanging sleeve if desired. Using the 2½"-wide blue plaid bias strips, prepare the binding and sew it to the quilt.

### COLOR OPTION

Because this pattern is so basic, it's versatile. It can be tailored to a baby theme, or created in fabrics specifically for a girl or boy of any age. It can be made in bright colors, reproduction prints, or holiday motifs—whatever fits the occasion. The possibilities are endless. I chose to do this variation in a cheery color combination with a fussy-cut border.

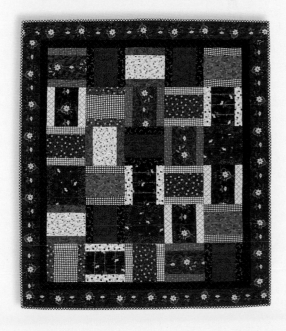

# Harvest Time

This pattern has been a bestseller among my designs. I personally love it because I have always found the fall colors to be so warm and inviting.

## Materials

*Yardage is based on 42"-wide fabric.*

2 yards *total* of assorted colors for blocks and outer border

1 yard of black plaid for blocks and binding

¾ yard of cream fabric for appliqué background

⅜ yard of black fabric for inner border

Assorted scraps in orange, green, gold, and brown for appliqué

3 yards of fabric for backing

52" x 52" piece of batting

¾ yard of fusible web

## Cutting

**From the assorted colors, cut:**
16 pieces, 2" x 8"
16 pieces, 2" x 6½"
16 pieces, 2" x 5"
16 pieces, 2" x 3½"
16 squares, 2" x 2"
40 squares, 4½" x 4½"

**From the cream fabric, cut:**
10 strips, 2" x 42"; crosscut into:
   16 pieces, 2" x 8"
   16 pieces, 2" x 6½"
   16 pieces, 2" x 5"
   16 pieces, 2" x 3½"
   16 squares, 2" x 2"

**From the black plaid, cut:**
5 strips, 2" x 42"; crosscut into 96 squares, 2" x 2"
4 squares, 4½" x 4½"
2½"-wide bias strips to total 210" in length

**From the black fabric, cut:**
4 strips, 2½" x 42"

## Making the Blocks

1. Sew a 2" colored square, a 2" cream square, and two 2" black plaid squares into a four-patch unit. Press the seams away from the black plaid. Sew a 3½" cream piece to the right side and a 3½" colored piece to the left side, pressing the seams toward these strips.

2. Sew a 2" black plaid square to one end of a 5" colored piece and sew this unit to the top of the block. Repeat with another 2" black plaid square and a 5" cream piece and sew this unit

Quilt size: 48½" x 48½"

to the bottom of the block so that the black squares form a diagonal line. Press the seams toward the strips at top and bottom. Sew a 6½" cream piece to the right side and a 6½" colored piece to the left side, pressing the seams toward these strips.

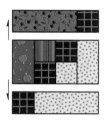 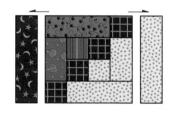

3. Sew a 2" black plaid square to one end of an 8" colored piece and sew this unit to the top of the block. Repeat with another 2" black plaid square and an 8" cream piece and sew this unit to the bottom of the block, pressing the seams toward these strips. Proof each block to 9½" x 9½".

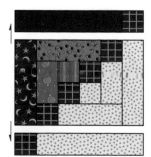 

Make 16.

24

## Assembling the Quilt-Top Center

1. Sew the blocks into four sections of four blocks each. Proof each section to 18½" x 18½".

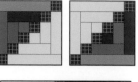 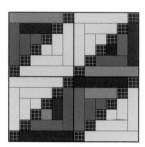

Make 4.

2. Referring to "Appliqué" on page 9, prepare the oak leaf and acorn appliqué shapes from the patterns on page 26. Fuse the shapes to the large cream area of each quilt section, referring to the photo at left for placement.

3. Machine appliqué the shapes using a blanket stitch with black topstitching thread.

4. Sew all four sections together as shown in the photo and proof the quilt-top center to 36½" x 36½". Repeat steps 2 and 3 with the pumpkin, stem, leaf, and vine appliqué shapes from the patterns on pages 26–27. You can also make the curlicue pumpkin stem by using a wide zigzag stitch. Refer to the photo for placement.

## Adding the Borders

Refer to "Adding the Borders" on page 8 for details as needed.

1. Cut two of the 2½"-wide black strips to a length of 36½" each and sew them to the sides of the quilt-top center. Cut the remaining two strips to a length of 40½" (piecing if needed) and sew these strips to the top and bottom of the quilt top. Press the seams toward the black borders. Proof the quilt top to 40½" x 40½".

2. Sew all the 4½" colored squares into four strips of 10 squares each. Press the seams in one direction. Sew two of these strips to the sides of the quilt top and press the seams toward the black inner borders. Add the 4½" black plaid squares to the ends of the remaining two strips and press as directed by the arrows. Sew these strips to the top and bottom of the quilt top and press the seams toward the black inner borders.

## Finishing the Quilt

Refer to the quilt-finishing techniques on pages 12–13, if needed.

1. Piece the quilt backing so that it's approximately 4" wider and longer than the quilt top. Mark the quilt top if necessary. Layer the quilt top with batting and backing, and baste the layers together. Hand or machine quilt as desired.

2. Trim the batting and backing even with the edges of the quilt top. Add a hanging sleeve if desired. Using the 2½"-wide black plaid bias strips, prepare the binding and sew it to the quilt.

### SIZE OPTION

To create this quilt in a smaller size, make four blocks as instructed for the larger quilt but switch the placement of the black and cream fabrics. Sew the blocks together with the black in the center. Cut a 5½" x 17" black rectangle and border it with 1¼"-wide orange strips. Sew this unit to the top of the blocks. For fun, I added a face to my pumpkin, turning it into a jack-o'-lantern. I used a pumpkin print to border this happy little quilt.

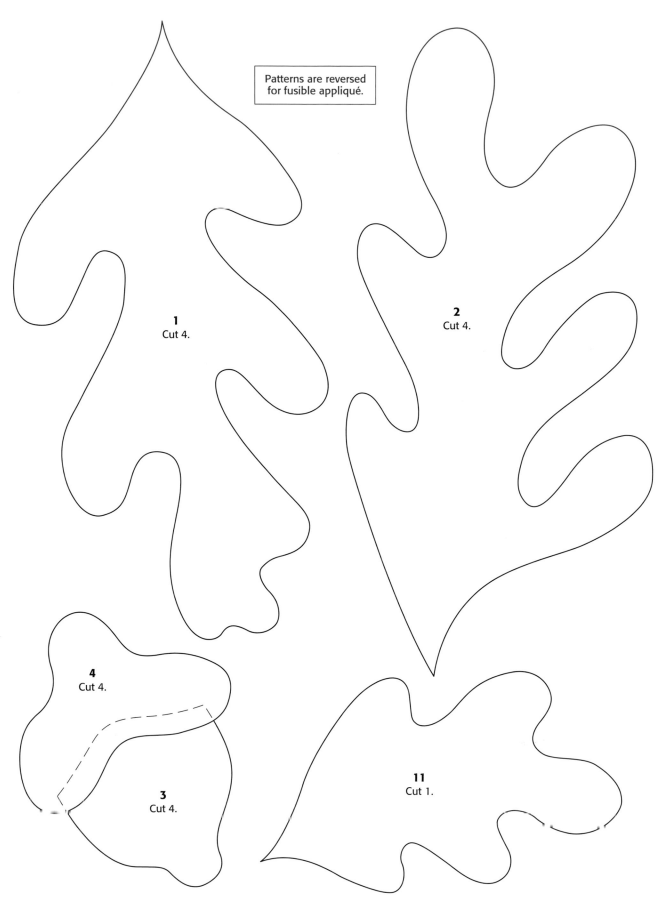

Patterns are reversed
for fusible appliqué.

**1**
Cut 4.

**2**
Cut 4.

**4**
Cut 4.

**3**
Cut 4.

**11**
Cut 1.

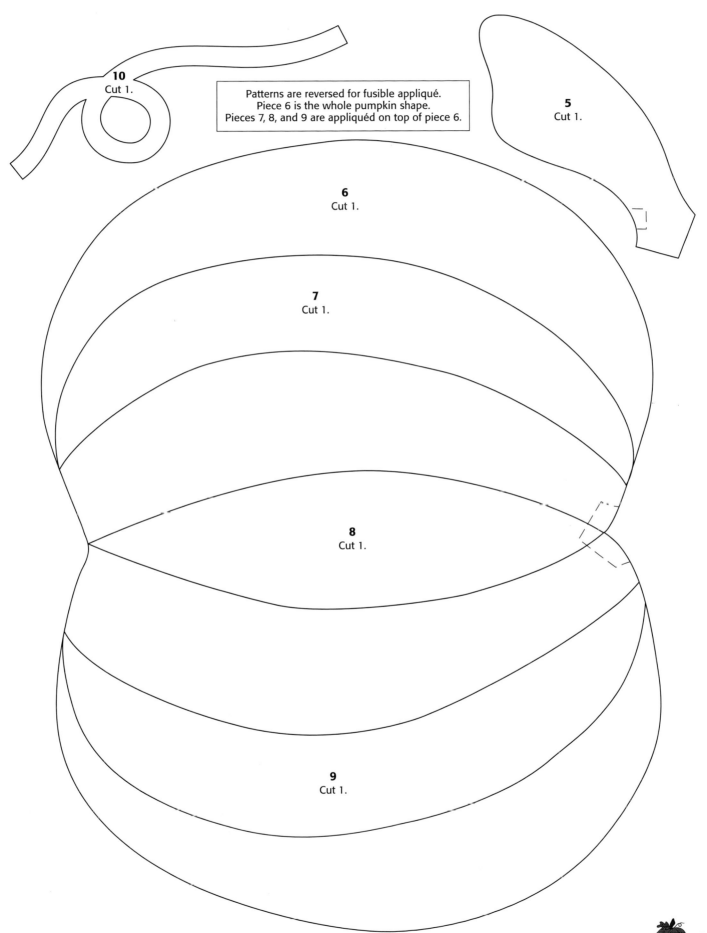

**10**
Cut 1.

**5**
Cut 1.

Patterns are reversed for fusible appliqué.
Piece 6 is the whole pumpkin shape.
Pieces 7, 8, and 9 are appliquéd on top of piece 6.

**6**
Cut 1.

**7**
Cut 1.

**8**
Cut 1.

**9**
Cut 1.

# Tiddlywinks

his is another one of those simple quilts that looks more complicated than it is. It's made of one simple block design, but when the blocks are sewn together they form a secondary block—the Hourglass. Well-planned pressing, detailed in the instructions, allows these intersections to nest easily.

## Materials

*Yardage is based on 42"-wide fabric.*

2 yards of cream fabric for blocks

⅝ yard of black fabric for blocks

⅝ yard of gold fabric for blocks

18 squares, 8" x 8", in assorted colors *or* 1 yard of a single fabric for blocks

Scraps of rust, blue, green, and gold for appliqué

⅝ yard of black plaid for binding

3 yards of fabric for backing

50" x 63" piece of batting

½ yard of fusible web

## Cutting

**From the gold fabric, cut:**
6 strips, 2½" x 42"; crosscut into 96 squares, 2½" x 2½"

**From the assorted colors (or single yard), cut:**
18 squares, 7" x 7"

**From the black fabric, cut:**
6 strips, 2½" x 42"; crosscut into 96 squares, 2½" x 2½"

**From the cream fabric, cut:**
9 strips, 7" x 42"; crosscut into 45 squares, 7" x 7"

**From the black plaid, cut**
2½"-wide bias strips to total 230" in length

## Making the Blocks

1. Referring to "Folded-Corner Units" on page 7, sew two 2½" gold squares to opposite corners of each 7" colored square. Press the seams toward the colored squares. Repeat on the remaining corners with two 2½" black squares and press the seams toward the black corners. Make 18.

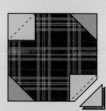 

Make 18.

Quilt size: 46" x 59"

2. Using the folded-corner technique, make the blocks shown with the 7" cream squares and the remaining 2½" gold squares and black squares. Continue pressing the seams toward the black and away from the gold.

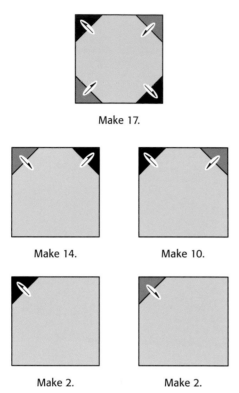

Make 17.

Make 14.    Make 10.

Make 2.    Make 2.

## Assembling the Quilt Top

1. Sew the blocks into seven rows of five blocks each as shown. Press the seams toward the colored squares. Sew the rows together, pressing the seams in either direction, and proof the quilt-top center to 33" x 46".

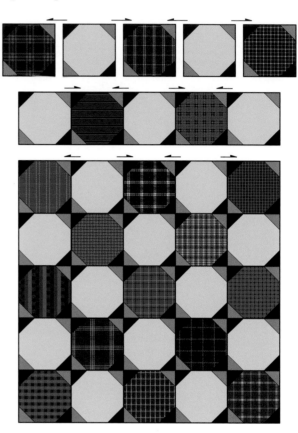

2. Sew the remaining cream blocks into rows as shown for border strips.

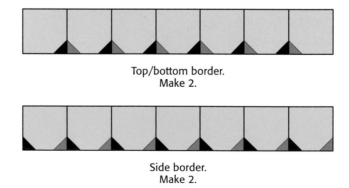

Top/bottom border.
Make 2.

Side border.
Make 2.

3. Referring to "Appliqué" on page 9, prepare the appliqué shapes from the patterns on page 32. Fuse the shapes to the pieced border strips, referring to the photo on page 29 for plaement.

4. Machine appliqué the stems, leaves, and gold flower centers using a zigzag stitch with matching thread. Feather-stitch the stars and blanket-stitch the red flowers using black topstitching thread. If your machine does not have a feather stitch, you can use a blanket stitch.

5. Referring to "Adding the Borders" on page 8 as needed, sew the side borders to the quilt-top center as shown, pressing the seams toward the borders. Sew the top and bottom borders to the quilt top and press the seams toward the borders.

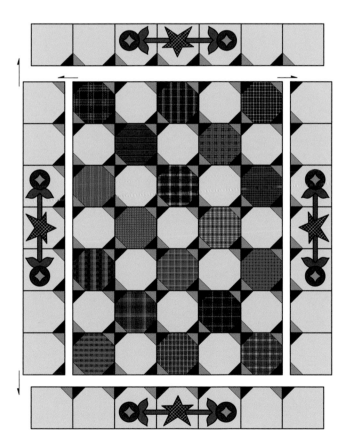

## Finishing

Refer to the quilt-finishing techniques on pages 12–13, if needed.

1. Piece the quilt backing so that it's approximately 4" wider and longer than the quilt top. Mark the quilt top if necessary. Layer the quilt top with batting and backing, and baste the layers together. Hand or machine quilt as desired.

2. Trim the batting and backing even with the edges of the quilt top. Cut off the corners of the quilt as shown in the photo on page 29. (Cut diagonally across each corner block.) Add a hanging sleeve if desired. Using the 2½"-wide black plaid bias strips, prepare the binding and sew it to the quilt.

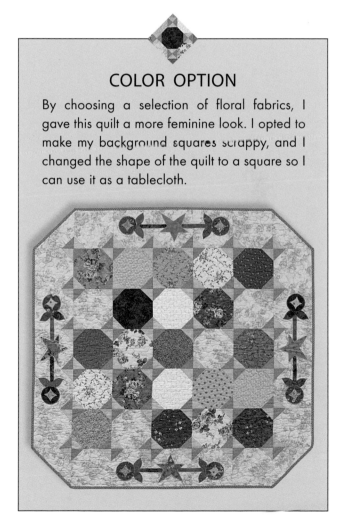

### COLOR OPTION

By choosing a selection of floral fabrics, I gave this quilt a more feminine look. I opted to make my background squares scrappy, and I changed the shape of the quilt to a square so I can use it as a tablecloth.

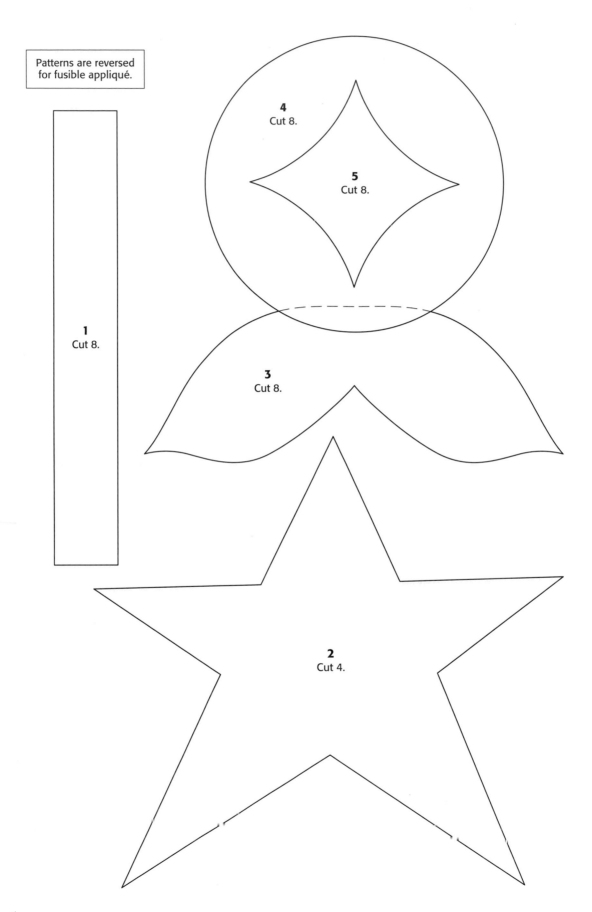

Patterns are reversed
for fusible appliqué.

**4**
Cut 8.

**5**
Cut 8.

**1**
Cut 8.

**3**
Cut 8.

**2**
Cut 4.

# Love Blooms

T his quilt is a great way to use up leftover strips, as the Log Cabin blocks are completely scrappy! Appliquéing a Log Cabin quilt usually involves working with the entire quilt at once, which can be cumbersome; but I added a touch of appliqué to the blocks before they were put together, making this project so much easier. Watch for this technique throughout the book—I use it as much as possible.

## Materials

*Yardage is based on 42"-wide fabric.*

2⅝ yards of black floral for outer border

10 fat quarters *or* 2½ yards *total* of assorted dark fabrics for blocks

10 fat quarters *or* 2½ yards *total* of assorted cream fabrics for blocks and sashing

1⅓ yards of black print for blocks, sashing, and inner border

⅞ yard of red fabric for pieced border and appliqué

¾ yard of gold fabric for pieced border and appliqué

¾ yard of blue fabric for middle border and appliqué

⅓ yard of green fabric for appliqué

⅛ yard of purple fabric for appliqué

1 yard of black stripe for binding

9 yards of fabric for backing

101" x 101" piece of batting

1¼ yards of fusible web

## Cutting

**From the black print, cut:**
18 strips, 2" x 42"; crosscut *10 strips* into:
   28 pieces, 2" x 11"
   24 squares, 2" x 2"
2 strips, 3⅞" x 42"; crosscut into 18 squares, 3⅞" x 3⅞"

**From the assorted cream fabrics\*, cut:**
32 pieces, 2" x 11"
36 pieces, 2" x 9½"
36 pieces, 2" x 8"
36 pieces, 2" x 6½"
36 pieces, 2" x 5"
18 squares, 3⅞" x 3⅞"
1 square, 2" x 2"

*\*If you're using 42"-wide yardage, you can cut the 2"-wide pieces from approximately thirty-six 2"-wide strips.*

Continued on page 35

Quilt size: 97" x 97"

**From the assorted dark fabrics\*\*, cut:**
36 pieces, 2" x 11"

36 pieces, 2" x 9½"

36 pieces, 2" x 8"

36 pieces, 2" x 6½"

36 pieces, 2" x 5"

36 pieces, 2" x 3½"

**From the gold fabric, cut:**
5 strips, 4⅜" x 42"; crosscut into 44 squares, 4⅜" x 4⅜"

**From the red fabric, cut:**
5 strips, 4⅜" x 42"; crosscut into 44 squares, 4⅜" x 4⅜"

**From the blue fabric, cut:**
9 strips, 1½" x 42"

**From the black floral, cut:**
10 strips, 7½" x 42"

**From the black stripe, cut:**
2½"-wide bias strips to total 400" in length

*\*\*If you're using 42"-wide yardage, you can cut these pieces from approximately forty 2"-wide strips.*

## Making the Blocks

1. Referring to "Half-Square-Triangle Units" on page 7, sew the 3⅞" black print squares and the 3⅞" cream squares together to make 36 half-square-triangle units. Press the seams toward the black and proof each unit to 3½" x 3½".

2. Sew the strips of cream and dark fabrics to the half-square-triangle units as shown. Start with the smallest dark strip on the bottom and add strips in a clockwise rotation, pressing all of the seams outward. Make 36 blocks and proof each block to 11" x 11".

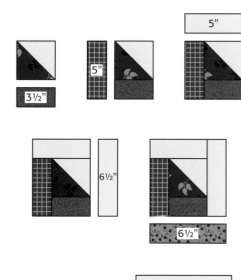

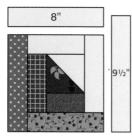

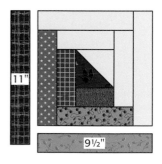

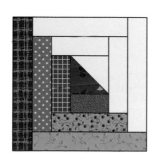

Make 36.

## Assembling the Quilt-Top Center

1. Lay out the 36 blocks, the 11" black print pieces, the 11" cream pieces, the 2" black print squares, and the 2" cream square as shown.

2. Sew the bolcks and other fabric pieces into rows as shown, pressing all seams toward the sashing pieces. Sew the rows together and press the seams toward the sashing pieces. Proof the quilt-top center to 71" x 71".

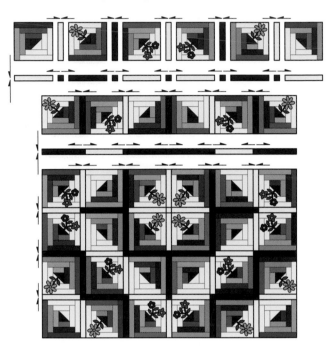

3. Referring to "Appliqué" on page 9, prepare the appliqué shapes from the patterns on page 38. Fuse shapes 1 through 4 to make the single flower design on 12 of the Log Cabin blocks, and fuse shapes 5 through 10 to make the double flower design on 12 more of the Log Cabin blocks. Refer to the photos above for placement, and keep the shapes close to the outer edge of each block without overlapping the ¼" seam allowance.

4. Machine appliqué the blue daisies using a blanket stitch with matching thread. Use a zigzag stitch with matching thread for the other shapes.

## Adding the Borders

Refer to "Adding the Borders" on page 8 for details as needed.

1. Sew the 2" black print strips together end to end. Cut off two lengths at 71" and sew them to the sides of the quilt-top center. Cut off two lengths at 74" and sew these to the top and bottom of the quilt top. Press all seams toward the black.

2. Referring to "Half-Square-Triangle Units" on page 7, sew the 4⅜" gold squares and the 4⅜" red squares together to make 88 half-square-triangle units. Press the seams toward the red and proof each unit to 4" x 4". Sew 21 of the units together as shown, pressing the seams in one direction, and proof each strip to a length of 74". Sew these strips to the sides of the quilt top and press the seams toward the black inner border. Sew the remaining units together as shown, pressing the seams in one direction, and proof each strip to a length of 81". Sew these strips to the top and bottom of the quilt top and press the seams toward the black inner border.

Side border.
Make 2.

Top/bottom border.
Make 2.

3. Sew the blue strips together end to end. Cut off two lengths at 81" and sew them to the sides of the quilt top. Cut off two lengths at 83" and sew them to the top and bottom of the quilt top. Press the seams toward the blue border.

4. Sew the black floral strips together end to end. Cut off two lengths at 83" and sew them to the sides of the quilt top. Cut off two lengths at 97" and sew them to the top and bottom of the quilt top. Press the seams toward the black floral border.

## Finishing

Refer to the quilt-finishing techniques on pages 12–13, if needed.

1. Piece the quilt backing so that it's approximately 4" wider and longer than the quilt top. Mark the quilt top if necessary. Layer the quilt top with batting and backing, and baste the layers together. Hand or machine quilt as desired.

2. Trim the batting and backing even with the edges of the quilt top. Add a hanging sleeve if desired. Using the 2½"-wide black stripe bias strips, prepare the binding and sew it to the quilt.

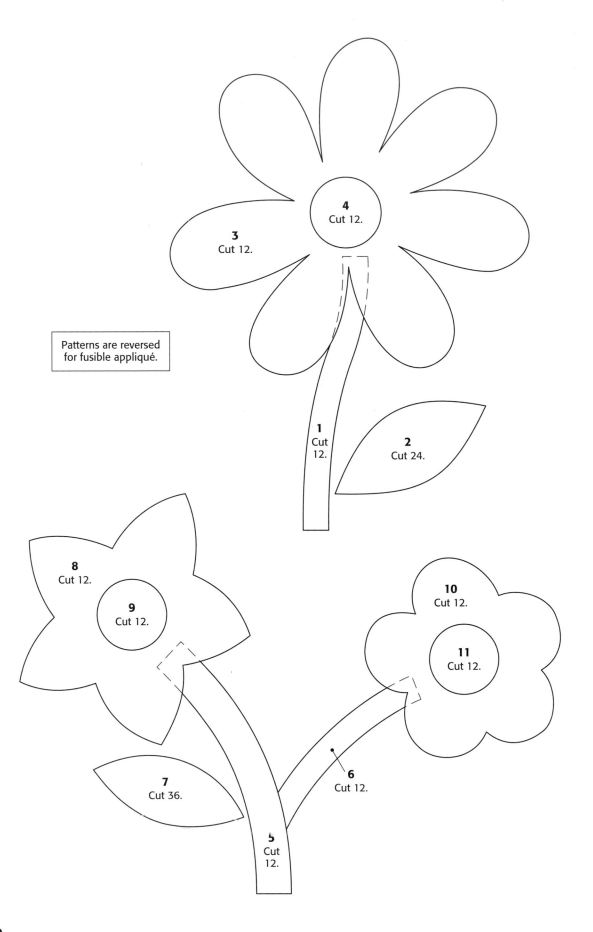

Patterns are reversed
for fusible appliqué.

3
Cut 12.

4
Cut 12.

1
Cut
12.

2
Cut 24.

8
Cut 12.

9
Cut 12.

10
Cut 12.

11
Cut 12.

7
Cut 36.

6
Cut 12.

5
Cut
12.

# Flower Boxes

This quilt is a longtime favorite of mine. I enjoy making Log Cabin blocks and I love how versatile this pattern is. It can have a primitive, contemporary, or traditional appearance depending on the fabrics chosen. Take a look at the quilt photos in "Color Options" on page 43 for more ideas.

## Materials

*Yardage is based on 42"-wide fabric.*

14 fat quarters *or* 3½ yards *total* of assorted plaids for blocks and appliqué

2⅜ yards of black plaid for background

½ yard of green fabric for appliqué

⅜ yard of black fabric for block centers

¾ yard of black plaid for binding

4 yards of fabric for backing

68" x 77" piece of batting

1 yard of fusible web

## Cutting

**From the assorted plaids, cut:**
20 sets* of:
   1 strip, 2" x 8"
   2 strips, 2" x 6½"
   1 strip, 2" x 5"
88 sets* of:
   1 strip, 2" x 5"
   2 strips, 2" x 3½"
   1 square, 2" x 2"

**From the black fabric, cut:**
5 strips, 2" x 42"; crosscut into 88 squares, 2" x 2"

**From the black plaid for background, cut:**
9 strips, 2" x 42"; crosscut into:
   12 strips, 2" x 8"
   24 strips, 2" x 6½"
   12 strips, 2" x 5"
3 strips, 6⅜" x 42"
3 strips, 5½" x 42"
4 squares, 12" x 12"; cut each square twice diagonally to yield 16 side triangles. (You will use 14.)
2 squares, 6½" x 6½"; cut each square once diagonally to yield 4 corner triangles

**From the black plaid for binding, cut:**
2½"-wide bias strips to total 290" in length

*\*Cut each set from 1 fabric for a consistent look within each block.*

Quilt size: 63½" x 72½"

## Making the Blocks

1. Choose one of the 88 assorted plaid sets and sew the 2" plaid square to a 2" black square. Press the seam toward the plaid. Continue adding the strips from the plaid set, working clockwise around the block. Press all the seams outward and proof each block to 5" x 5".

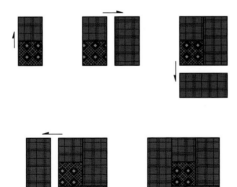

Make 88.

2. Pick an assortment of 20 blocks from step 1. Choose one of the 20 assorted plaid sets and sew a 5" plaid strip to the top of a block. Press the seam outward. Continue adding the strips from this set, working clockwise around the block. Press all the seams outward and proof each block to 8" x 8".

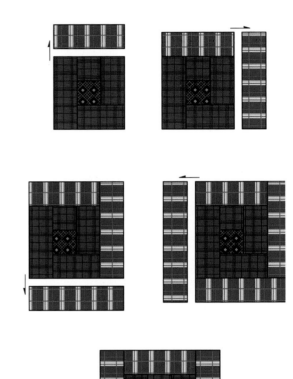

Make 20.

3. Pick an assortment of 12 blocks from step 1 and repeat step 2 using the 2"-wide black plaid background strips. Proof each block to 8" x 8".

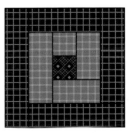

Make 12.

## Assembling the Quilt Top

1. Lay out the blocks from steps 2 and 3 along with the black side and corner triangles as shown. Sew the blocks and side triangles into rows. Press all seams toward the black plaid. Sew the rows together and press the seams in either direction. Add the corner triangles and press the seams toward the triangles. Proof the quilt-top center to 42⅞" x 53½", trimming so the block points are ¼" from the edge.

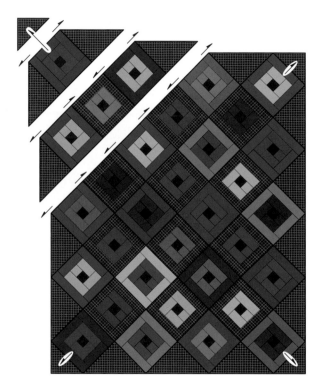

2. Referring to "Adding the Borders" on page 8 as needed, sew the 6⅜" black plaid strips together end to end. Cut off two lengths at 53½" for the side borders. Sew the 5½" black plaid strips together end to end. Cut off two lengths at 54⅝" for the top and bottom borders.

3. Referring to "Appliqué" on page 9, prepare the appliqué shapes from the patterns on page 44. Arrange the flowers on the border strips, as close to the strip edges as possible without overlapping the ¼" seam allowance. Lay each border strip next to the quilt-top center to make sure the flowers are centered and in the right place (about 10⅝" apart); you can also refer to the photo on page 41 for placement. Fuse the shapes to the border strips.

4. Machine appliqué the stems and leaves using a small zigzag stitch with green thread, and blanket-stitch the flowers with black topstitching thread. Sew the side borders to the sides of the quilt-top center, and then sew the top and bottom borders to the quilt top. Press all the seams toward the black plaid border. Proof the quilt top to 54½" x 63½".

5. Sew together the remaining blocks from step 1 to make four strips of 14 blocks each. Sew two of these strips to the sides of the quilt top and the remaining two strips to the top and bottom. Press the seams toward the black plaid border.

Make 4.

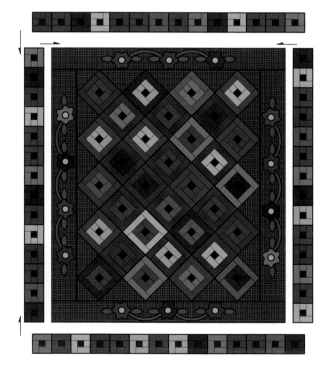

## Finishing

Refer to the quilt-finishing techniques on pages 12–13, if needed.

1. Piece the quilt backing so that it's approximately 4" wider and longer than the quilt top. Mark the quilt top if necessary. Layer the quilt top with batting and backing, and baste the layers together. Hand or machine quilt as desired.

2. Trim the batting and backing even with the edges of the quilt top. Add a hanging sleeve if desired. Using the 2½"-wide black plaid bias strips, prepare the binding and sew it to the quilt.

## COLOR OPTIONS

This first quilt variation was contributed by my mom, Deb. She chose to do a fairly traditional rendition of the design by using a cream background and a selection of small floral prints.

I, on the other hand, went for a more contemporary style, not only in my fabric choices but in the very shape of my quilt. By leaving off the setting triangles and borders, I allowed the black binding to reveal some dramatic points.

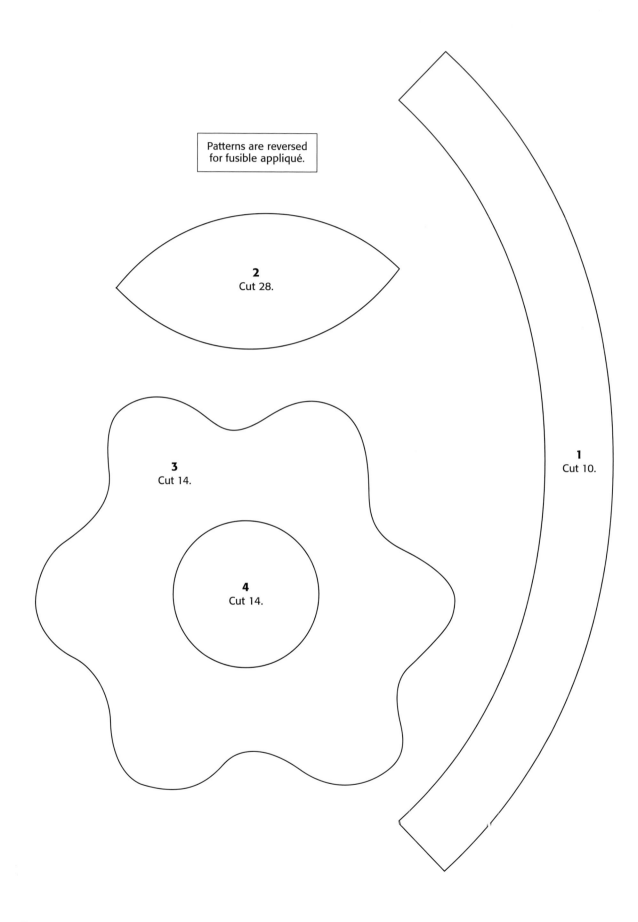

Patterns are reversed
for fusible appliqué.

**2**
Cut 28.

**3**
Cut 14.

**4**
Cut 14.

**1**
Cut 10.

# Rickrack Roses

This quilt includes some of my favorite tricks for simplifying the piecing process. First, the strip-pieced checkerboards have offset intersections, so there's no seam matching! Also, the easy lattice strips are just jumbo rickrack, eliminating the need to sew extra seams.

## Materials

*Yardage is based on 42"-wide fabric.*

12 fat quarters of assorted colors for blocks and appliqué

1 yard of blue floral for outer border

⅞ yard of cream fabric for middle border

⅛ yard *each* of 5 pink prints *or* ⅜ yard *total* of 1 pink print for checkerboard border

⅓ yard of green plaid for inner border

¼ yard *total* of assorted green fabrics for appliqué

⅝ yard of pink plaid for binding

3 yards of fabric for backing

54" x 63" piece of batting

¾ yard of fusible web

275" of jumbo white rickrack

## Cutting

**From *each* of the fat quarters, cut:**
1 square, 9" x 9"

**From the green plaid, cut:**
4 strips, 2" x 42"

**From the cream fabric, cut:**
5 strips, 1¾" x 42"
9 strips, 2" x 42"

**From the pink print(s), cut:**
5 strips, 2¼" x 42"

**From the blue floral, cut:**
6 strips, 5" x 42"

**From the pink plaid, cut:**
2½"-wide bias strips to total 230" in length

## Assembling the Quilt-Top Center

1. Referring to "Appliqué" on page 9, prepare the appliqué shapes from the patterns on page 49. Fuse the shapes to the 9" colored squares, referring to the photo on page 48 for placement. Machine appliqué the shapes using a blanket stitch with black topstitching thread.

2. Sew the blocks into four rows of three blocks each. Press the seams in opposite directions from row to row. Sew the rows together, pressing the seams in either direction, and proof the quilt-top center to 26" x 34½". Measure, cut, and pin the rickrack horizontally between the rows, and then stitch in place with matching thread. Repeat to sew rickrack vertically between the rows.

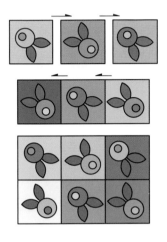

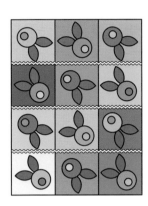

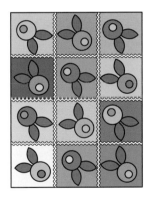

## Adding the Borders

Refer to "Adding the Borders" on page 8 for details as needed.

1. Cut two of the 2" green plaid strips to a length of 34½" and sew them to the sides of the quilt-top center. Press the seams toward the green plaid. Cut the remaining two strips to a length of 29" and sew these to the top and bottom of the quilt top. Again, press the seams toward the green plaid. Proof the quilt top to 29" x 37½".

2. Sew rickrack around the perimeter of the quilt-top center as shown in the photo. Tuck under any raw edges and use a fray-deterring product if desired.

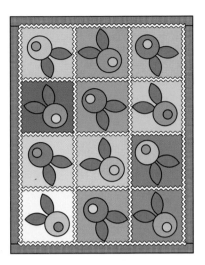

3. Using four of the 2" cream strips, cut off two lengths at 37½" and sew them to the sides of the quilt top. Press the seams toward the green plaid. Cut off two lengths at 32" and sew these to the top and bottom of the quilt top, again pressing toward the green plaid. Proof the quilt top to 32" x 40½".

4. Sew the 1¾" cream strips and the 2¼" pink strips together along their long edges to make five strip sets as shown. Cut the strip sets into 84 segments, 2¼" wide, and 4 segments, 2⅝" wide.

Make 5 strip sets.
Cut 84 segments, 2¼" wide.
Cut 4 segments, 2⅝" wide.

5. Make two strips for the side borders by sewing 23 of the 2¼"-wide segments together as shown. Trim ⅛" from each end of each strip as shown. Proof each strip to a length of 40½". Sew these strips to the sides of the quilt

Quilt size: 50" x 58½"

top, referring to the diagram on page 49 for placement, and press the seams toward the cream border.

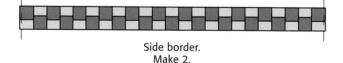

Side border.
Make 2.

6. Make two strips for the top and bottom borders by sewing 19 of the 2¼"-wide segments together. Add one 2⅝"-wide segment to each end of each strip. Proof each strip to a length of 38". Sew these strips to the top and bottom of the

quilt top, referring to the diagram on page 49 for placement, and press the seams toward the cream border.

Top/bottom border.
Make 2.

7. Sew the remaining 2" cream strips together end to end. Cut two strips to a length of 46½" and sew them to the sides of the quilt top. Press the seams toward the newly added strips. Cut two more strips to a length of 41" and sew these to the top and bottom of the quilt top.

Press the seams toward the newly added strips and proof the quilt top to 41" x 49½".

8. Sew the 5" blue print strips together end to end. Cut off two lengths at 49½" and sew them to the sides of the quilt top. Cut off two lengths at 50" and sew these to the top and bottom of the quilt. Press all the seams toward the blue print.

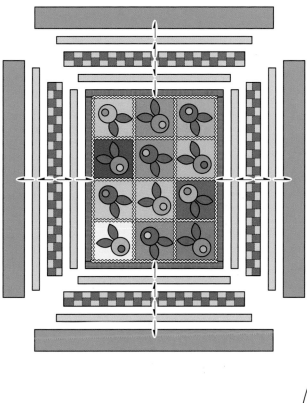

## Finishing

Refer to the quilt-finishing techniques on pages 12–13, if needed.

1. Piece the quilt backing so that it's approximately 4" wider and longer than the quilt top. Mark the quilt top if necessary. Layer the quilt top with batting and backing, and baste the layers together. Hand or machine quilt as desired.

2. Trim the batting and backing even with the edges of the quilt top. Add a hanging sleeve if desired. Using the 2½"-wide pink plaid bias strips, prepare the binding and sew it to the quilt.

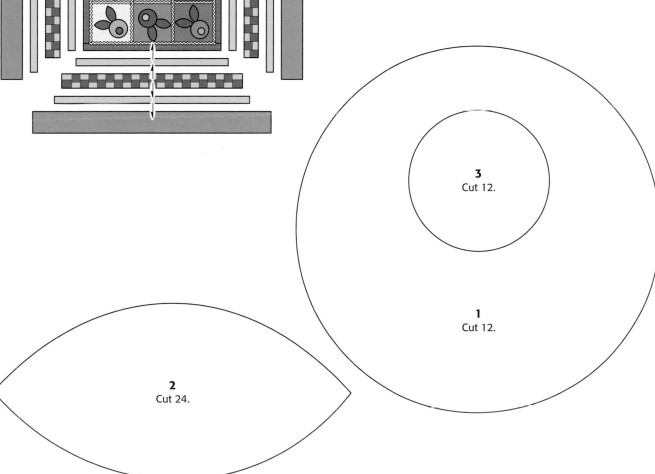

**3**
Cut 12.

**1**
Cut 12.

**2**
Cut 24.

# Candy Apple Blossoms

This quilt features another variation of the Log Cabin block. The look of gently curved piecing is created just by varying the width of the strips. Focus on the individual "logs" and notice how the cream strips are 1" wide while the colored strips are 1½" wide. Now look again at the Log Cabin block as a whole and you will fully appreciate its secret—no curved piecing required!

## Materials

*Yardage is based on 42"-wide fabric.*

1⅞ yards of cream fabric for background

1½ yards of red floral for outer border

1 yard *total* of red, green, and pink fabrics for blocks

½ yard of green fabric for inner border and appliqué

⅛ yard *each* of 2 red prints, 1 green dot fabric, and 1 gold fabric for appliqué

¾ yard of green stripe for binding

4 yards of fabric for backing

66" x 66" piece of batting

1 yard of fusible web

## Cutting

**From the red, green, and pink fabrics\* for blocks, cut a *total* of:**

32 pieces, 1½" x 5½"

32 pieces, 1½" x 4½"

32 pieces, 1½" x 4"

32 pieces, 1½" x 3"

32 pieces, 1½" x 2½"

32 squares, 1½" x 1½"

**From the cream fabric, cut:**

2 strips, 1½" x 42"; crosscut into 32 squares, 1½" x 1½"

22 strips, 1" x 42"; crosscut into:

    32 pieces, 1" x 6"

    32 pieces, 1" x 5½"

    32 pieces, 1" x 4½"

    32 pieces, 1" x 4"

    32 pieces, 1" x 3"

    32 pieces, 1" x 2½"

3 strips, 11½" x 42"; crosscut into:

    5 squares, 11½" x 11½"

    4 rectangles, 6" x 11½"

    4 squares, 6" x 6"

*\*If you're using 42"-wide yardage, you can cut these pieces from approximately eighteen 1½"-wide strips.*

Continued on page 53

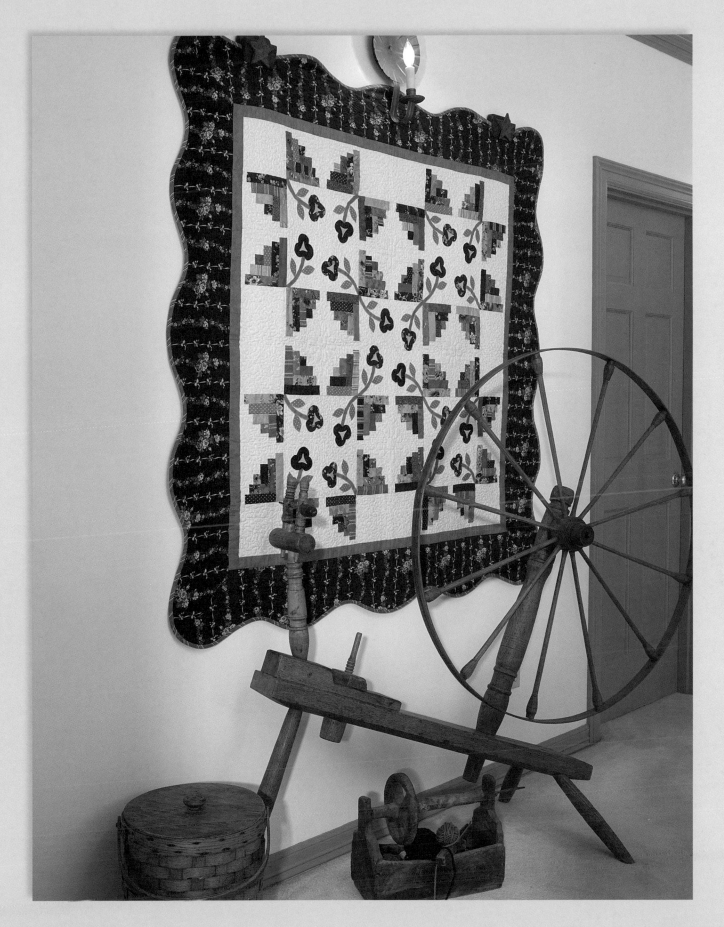

Quilt size: 62" x 62"

Designed by Deb Mulder

From the green fabric, cut:
5 strips, 1¾" x 42"

From the red floral, cut:
6 strips, 8" x 42"

From the green stripe, cut:
2½"-wide bias strips to total 265" in length

## Making the Blocks

1. Sew each 1½" red, green, and pink square to a 1½" cream square. Press toward the colored squares. Sew a colored strip to the bottom of the unit. Sew a cream strip to the right side. Continue adding the strips around the block counterclockwise, pressing all seams outward. Make 32 blocks and proof each block to 6" x 6".

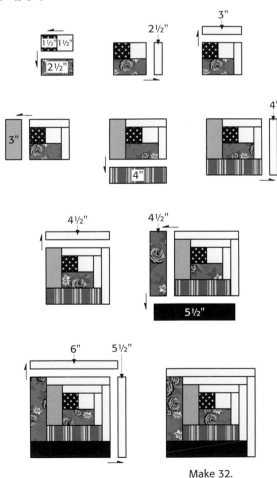

Make 32.

2. Sew 16 of the blocks into pairs as shown. Press the seam in either direction. Sew the remaining 16 blocks into 4 large blocks. Press the seams in either direction.

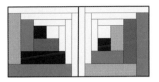

Make 8.

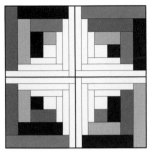

Make 4.

3. Referring to "Appliqué" on page 9, prepare the appliqué shapes from the patterns on page 56. Fuse the shapes to the 11½" cream squares, referring to the photo on page 52 for placement. Machine appliqué the red flowers using a blanket stitch with matching thread, and use a small zigzag stitch with matching thread for the leaves, stems, and flower centers.

## Assembling the Quilt Top

1. Lay out the Log Cabin blocks, the appliqué blocks, and the cream rectangles and squares as shown. Sew the pieces into rows and press all the seams away from the pieced blocks. Sew the rows together, pressing the seams in either direction, and proof the quilt-top center to 44½" x 44½".

2. Referring to "Adding the Borders" on page 8 as needed, sew the 1¾"-wide green strips together end to end. Cut off two lengths at 44½" and sew them to the sides of the quilt-top center. Press the seams toward the green. Cut off two lengths at 47" and sew these to the top and bottom of the quilt top. Again, press the seams toward the green.

3. Sew the red floral strips together end to end. Cut off two lengths at 47" and sew them to the sides of the quilt top. Press the seams toward the red. Cut off two lengths at 62" and sew these to the top and bottom of the quilt top. Again, press the seams toward the red. Note that if you are using a striped border fabric, you may want to miter the corners of the quilt top as I did. The two quilts shown in "Color Options" on page 55 have borders with straight-cut corners.

## Finishing

Refer to the quilt-finishing techniques on pages 12–13, if needed.

1. Piece the quilt backing so that it's approximately 4" wider and longer than the quilt top. Mark the quilt top if necessary. If you wish to scallop your border, the scallop patterns are on page 57. Mark the scallop designs on the borders before quilting, and trim along the lines after quilting. Layer the quilt top with batting and backing, and baste the layers together. Hand or machine quilt as desired.

2. Trim the batting and backing even with the edges of the quilt top. Add a hanging sleeve if desired. Using the 2½"-wide green stripe bias strips, prepare the binding and sew it to the quilt.

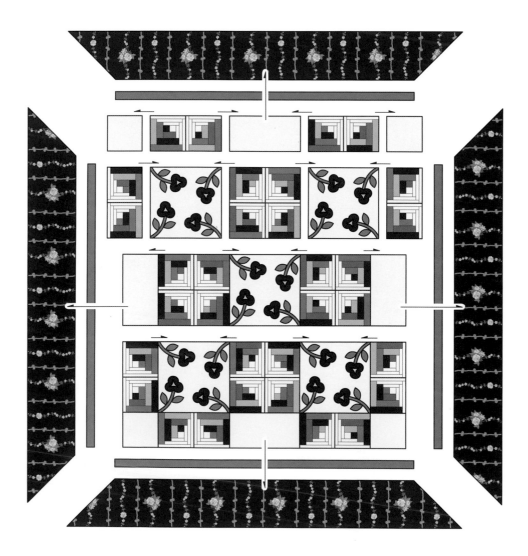

## COLOR OPTIONS

These quilts show two extremes—one is primitive, using all woven plaids and felted-wool appliqué, while the other has a "cottage" look created with soft floral prints.

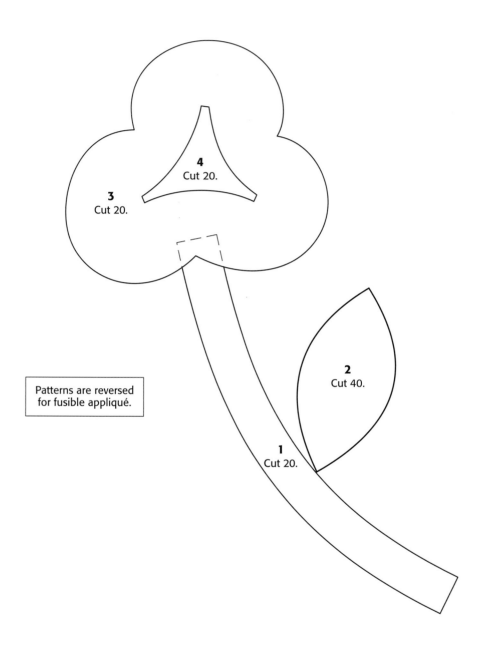

**4**
Cut 20.

**3**
Cut 20.

Patterns are reversed
for fusible appliqué.

**2**
Cut 40.

**1**
Cut 20.

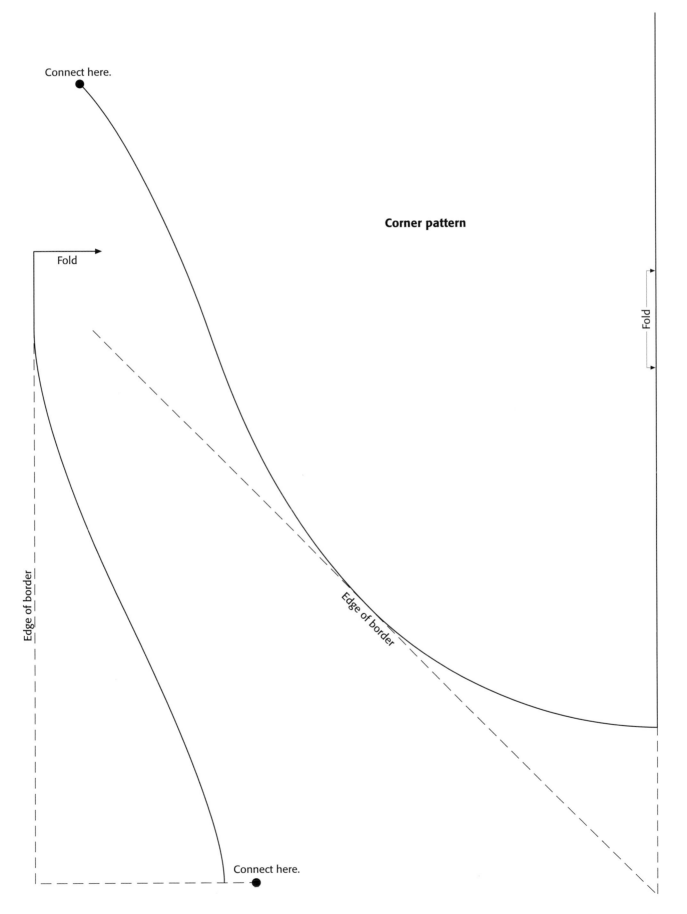

Connect here.

**Corner pattern**

Fold

Fold

Edge of border

Edge of border

Connect here.

# Christmas Glow

Ilove Christmas quilts and believe that every home needs a few. This versatile quilt can be used as a table topper, or you can cut a hole in the center and use it as a tree skirt.

## Materials

*Yardage is based on 42"-wide fabric.*

1⅛ yards of red print for checkerboards, outer borders, and binding

½ yard of gold fabric for star points and candle flames

½ yard of purple fabric for star background

⅓ yard of cream print for checkerboards

⅓ yard of black solid for holly blocks

1 fat quarter of black print for candle blocks

¼ yard of green fabric for holly and candleholders

3 yards of fabric for backing

51" x 51" piece of batting

½ yard of fusible web

## Cutting

**From the red print, cut:**
8 strips, 2¼" x 42"; crosscut into:
 3 pieces, 2¼" x 18"
 4 pieces, 2¼" x 14"
 4 pieces, 2¼" x 12"
 4 pieces, 2¼" x 11"
 4 pieces, 2¼" x 9¼"
 4 pieces, 2¼" x 7½"
5 strips, 2½" x 42"

**From the cream print, cut:**
3 strips, 2¼" x 42"; crosscut into:
 4 pieces, 2¼" x 18"
 3 pieces, 2¼" x 11"

**From the gold fabric, cut:**
2 strips, 6⅝" x 42"; crosscut into 8 squares, 6⅝" x 6⅝"

**From the purple fabric, cut:**
4 rectangles, 7½" x 12¾"

**From the green fabric, cut:**
4 squares, 4" x 4"

**From the black print, cut:**
4 squares, 7½" x 7½"

**From the black solid, cut:**
2 squares, 9½" x 9½"

## Making the Blocks

1. Sew the 11"-long red print and cream print strips together along the long edges as shown, pressing the seams toward the red. Cut this strip set into four segments, 2¼" wide.

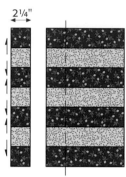

Make 1 strip set.
Cut 4 segments.

2. Sew the 18"-long red print and cream print strips together along the long edges as shown, pressing the seams toward the red. Cut this strip set into seven segments, 2¼" wide.

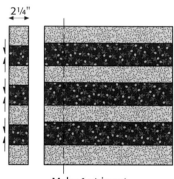

Make 1 strip set.
Cut 7 segments.

3. Sew the segments from step 1 and three segments from step 2 together as shown and proof the block to 12¾" x 12¾".

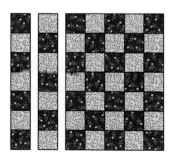

Make 1.

4. Referring to "Folded-Corner Units" on page 7, sew two gold squares to each purple rectangle. Press the seams toward the gold. Sew one of the remaining strip-set segments from step 2 to each block as shown and press toward the red-and-cream segments.

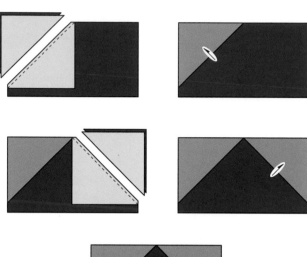

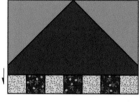

Make 4.

5. Again using the folded-corner technique, sew a green square to a corner of each black print square. Press the seam toward the green. With the triangle at lower left, sew a 7½" red print strip to the left side of each block, pressing the seam toward the red. Sew a 9¼" red print strip to the bottom and press the seam toward the red.

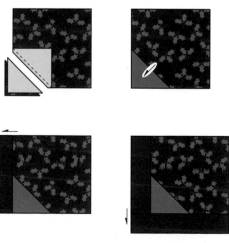

Make 4.

Quilt size: 46½" at the widest point

6. Draw a diagonal line on each of the 9½" black solid squares. Sew ⅛" from both sides of the line and cut on the drawn line. (This is done to help stabilize the bias edge while the block is machine appliquéd.) Sew a 12" red print strip to the left side of each triangle as shown and press the seam toward the red. Sew a 14" red print strip to the other side, press the seam toward the red, and trim the strips even with the bottom of the triangle.

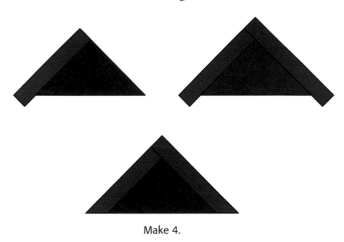

Make 4.

7. Referring to "Appliqué" on page 9, prepare the appliqué shapes from the patterns on page 63. Fuse the shapes to the blocks from steps 5 and 6 as shown in the photo on page 61. Machine appliqué the flame and candle using a small zigzag stitch in matching thread, and appliqué everything else using a blanket stitch with black topstitching thread.

## Assembling the Quilt Top

1. Lay out the checkerboard block and the blocks from steps 4 and 5 of the preceding section as shown. Sew the blocks into rows, pressing the seams as directed by the arrows (see diagram below). Sew the rows together and press as directed.

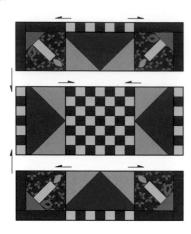

2. Add the triangle units, pressing the seams as directed.

## Finishing

Refer to the quilt-finishing techniques on pages 12–13, if needed.

1. Piece the quilt backing so that it's approximately 4" wider and longer than the quilt top. Mark the quilt top if necessary. Layer the quilt top with batting and backing, and baste the layers together. Hand or machine quilt as desired.

2. Trim the batting and backing even with the edges of the quilt top. Add a hanging sleeve if desired. Using the 2½"-wide red print strips, prepare the binding and sew it to the quilt.

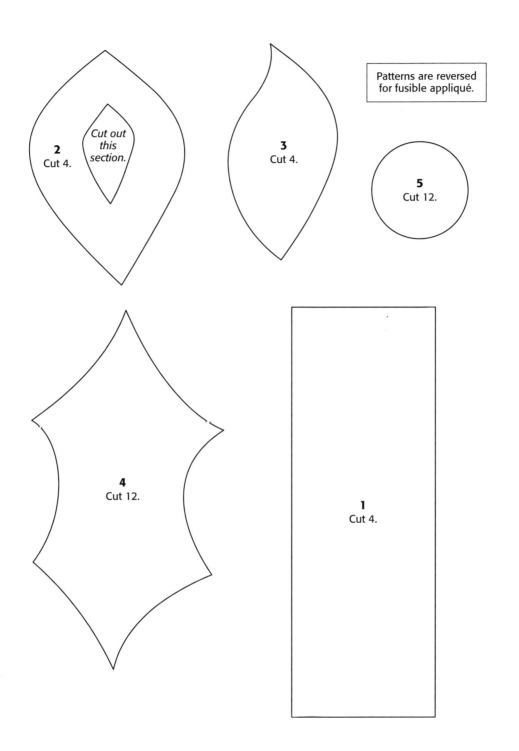

Patterns are reversed
for fusible appliqué.

**2**
Cut 4.

*Cut out
this
section.*

**3**
Cut 4.

**5**
Cut 12.

**4**
Cut 12.

**1**
Cut 4.

# Scrappy Stars

I'm partial to this quilt because it combines two of my favorite things—stars and chains. It's a great way to use up your scraps, as the background for each block takes very little fabric.

## Materials

*Yardage is based on 42"-wide fabric.*

24 fat eighths *or* large scraps of assorted fabrics for star backgrounds

¾ yard *total* of assorted yellow fabrics for star points

⅝ yard of black plaid for chain

⅝ yard of black print for outer border

¼ yard of cream fabric for star centers

¾ yard of black plaid for binding

2⅝ yards of fabric for backing

46" x 64" piece of batting

## Cutting

**From the black plaid for chain, cut:**
3 strips, 2" x 42"
5 strips, 2" x 42"; crosscut into 96 squares, 2" x 2"

**From the cream fabric, cut:**
3 strips, 2" x 42"

**From the yellow fabrics\*, cut:**
192 squares, 2" x 2"

*\*If you'd like to cut the yellow squares from yardage, you'll need ten 2" x 42" strips.*

**From the assorted fabrics for star backgrounds, cut:**
24 sets\*\* of:
   2 pieces, 2" x 8"
   2 pieces, 2" x 6½"
   4 pieces, 2" x 3½"
   2 squares, 2" x 2"

**From the black print, cut:**
5 strips, 3¼" x 42"

**From the black plaid for binding, cut:**
2½"-wide bias strips to total 215" in length

*\*\*Cut each set from 1 fabric for a consistent look within each block.*

## Making the Blocks

1. Sew the 2" black plaid strips and cream strips into three pairs, pressing the seams toward the black. Cut into 48 segments, 2" wide. Sew the segments together to make 24 four-patch units and proof each unit to 3½" x 3½".

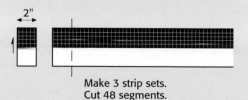

Make 3 strip sets.
Cut 48 segments.

Make 24.

Quilt size: 42" x 60"

2. Referring to "Folded-Corner Units" on page 7, sew two yellow squares to each of the 2" x 3½" pieces from the assorted-fabric sets as shown. Press the seams toward the yellow.

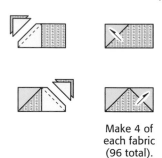

Make 4 of
each fabric
(96 total).

3. Using the four-patch units from step 1, the flying-geese units from step 2, the black plaid squares, and the matching squares from each set, sew the blocks together. Press as directed by the arrows.

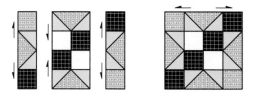

4. Sew the matching 2" x 6½" pieces to the sides of each block and press the seams away from the center. Sew one of the remaining black plaid squares to each of the 2" x 8" assorted pieces, pressing away from the black plaid. Sew these to the top and bottom of each block, matching the background fabric. Again, press the seams away from the center. Proof each block to 9½" x 9½".

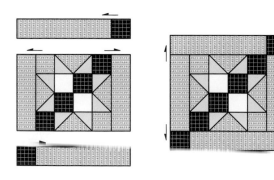

## Assembling the Quilt Top

1. Lay out the blocks into six rows of four blocks each. Sew the blocks into rows, pressing the seams in opposite directions from row to row. Sew the rows together, pressing the seams in either direction, and proof the quilt-top center to 36½" x 54½".

2. Referring to "Adding the Borders" on page 8 as needed, sew the black print strips together end to end. Cut off two strips at 54½" and sew them to the sides of the quilt-top center. Press the seams toward the border. Cut off two strips at 42" and sew these to the top and bottom of the quilt top. Press the seams toward the border.

## Finishing

Refer to the quilt-finishing techniques on pages 12–13, if needed.

1. Piece the quilt backing so that it's approximately 4" wider and longer than the quilt top. Mark the quilt top if necessary. Layer the quilt top with batting and backing, and baste the layers together. Hand or machine quilt as desired.

2. Trim the batting and backing even with the edges of the quilt top. Add a hanging sleeve if desired. Using the 2½"-wide black plaid bias strips, prepare the binding and sew it to the quilt.

## COLOR OPTION

For this quilt, I started with the black floral fabric, and then chose coordinating prints for the star blocks. The result is this rich combination.

# April Showers

*D*o you want curved borders on your quilt, but don't want the challenge of binding around them? Here I have appliquéd half circles to the outer-border strips before sewing the strips to the quilt. The result is the same effect—it's just much easier.

## Materials

*Yardage is based on 42"-wide fabric.*

1¼ yards of yellow floral for outer border

1 yard of red check for blocks and binding

⅞ yard of cream fabric for background

⅝ yard of red print for scallops and appliqué

½ yard of yellow print for blocks and appliqué

½ yard of green dot for inner border

Scraps of blue, pink, red, and green for appliqué

3 yards of fabric for backing

50" x 60" piece of batting

1½ yards of fusible web

## Cutting

**From the yellow print, cut:**
8 strips, 1½" x 42"

**From the red check, cut:**
5 strips, 1½" x 42"
2½"-wide bias strips to total 210" in length

**From the cream fabric, cut:**
3 strips, 1½" x 42"

1 strip, 2½" x 42"; crosscut into 12 squares, 2½" x 2½"

3 squares, 9¾" x 9¾"; cut each square twice diagonally to yield 12 side triangles. (You will use 10.)

2 squares, 5¼" x 5¼"; cut each square once diagonally to yield 4 corner triangles

6 squares, 6½" x 6½"

**From the green dot, cut:**
2 strips, 2⅜" x 42"; crosscut into 28 squares, 2⅜" x 2⅜". Cut each square once diagonally to yield 56 triangles.

3 strips, 3⅜" x 42"; crosscut into:
  14 pieces, 3⅜" x 6⅛"
  4 squares, 3⅜" x 3⅜"

**From the yellow floral, cut:**
5 strips, 7½" x 42"

## Making the Blocks

1. Sew five of the yellow print strips and the red check strips into strip sets as shown. Press the seams toward the yellow. Cut into 124 segments, 1½" wide. Sew the segments together to make 62 four-patch units. Proof each unit to 2½" x 2½".

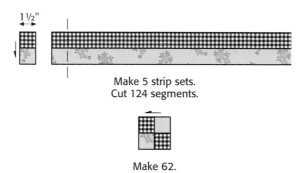

Make 5 strip sets.
Cut 124 segments.

Make 62.

2. Sew the remaining yellow print strips and the 1½" cream strips into three strip sets as shown. Press the seams toward the yellow. Cut into 48 segments, 2½" wide.

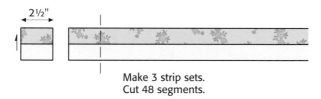

Make 3 strip sets.
Cut 48 segments.

3. Sew the units from steps 1 and 2 together with the 2½" cream squares as shown. Set aside the leftover four-patch units for the inner border. Press the seams toward the step 2 units. Make 12 blocks and proof each block to 6½" x 6½".

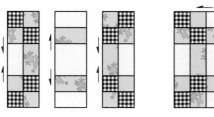

Make 12.

## Assembling the Quilt-Top Center

1. Lay out six of the pieced blocks, three 6½" cream squares, five side triangles, and two corner triangles as shown. Sew the blocks into rows, pressing the seams toward the cream fabric. Sew the rows together and press the seams in either direction. Repeat to make two of these large triangle sections.

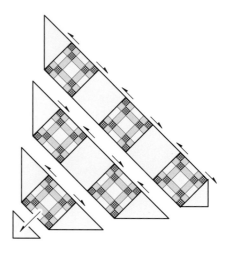

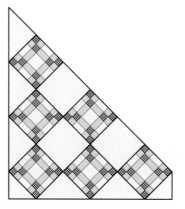

Make 2.

2. Referring to "Appliqué" on page 9, prepare the appliqué shapes from the patterns on pages 73–74. Referring to the photo on page 71, position the shapes on one of the triangles. Machine appliqué the green stems and yellow flower centers using a small zigzag stitch with matching thread, and appliqué the remaining shapes using a blanket stitch with black topstitching thread. After the appliqué is done, sew the two triangles together. Proof the quilt-top center to 26" x 34½".

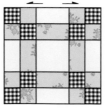

Quilt size: 45¾" x 54¼"

## Adding the Borders

Refer to "Adding the Borders" on page 8 as needed.

1. Sew the green dot triangles to opposite sides of the four-patch units you set aside in step 3 of "Making the Blocks." Press the seams toward the green. Add a triangle to each of the remaining sides, press, and proof each block to 3⅜" x 3⅜".

Make 14.

2. Sew the blocks from step 1, the 6⅛"-long green dot pieces, and the 3⅜" green dot squares into strips, pressing the seams away from the blocks.

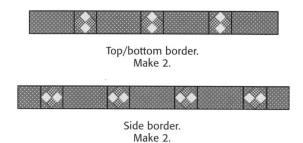

Top/bottom border.
Make 2.

Side border.
Make 2.

3. Sew the longer rows to the sides of the quilt-top center, pressing the seam toward the inner border. Then sew the shorter rows to the top and bottom of the quilt top and press the seams toward the inner border. Proof the quilt top to 31¾" x 40¼".

4. Cut two of the yellow floral strips into lengths of 40¼" (piecing as needed). Prepare the scallop shapes from the patterns on page 75. Lay the border strips next to the sides of the quilt top and position the red scallops as shown in the photo on page 71. The small scallops are at each end and the large scallops are in the center of each strip. The points of the scallops should meet at the tip of the four-patch units. Fuse the scallops in place and machine appliqué using a blanket stitch with black topstitching thread. Sew these strips to the

sides of the quilt top, pressing the seams toward the green dot border. Sew the remaining yellow floral strips together end to end and cut off two lengths at 45¾". Repeat the procedure for adding scallops, and sew these top and bottom border strips to the quilt top.

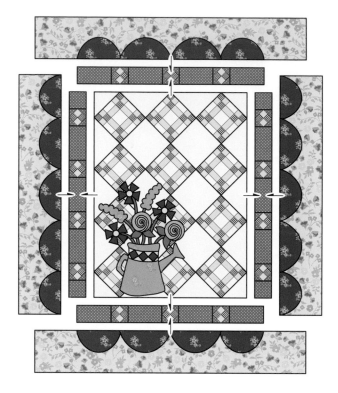

## Finishing

Refer to the quilt-finishing techniques on pages 12–13, if needed.

1. Piece the quilt backing so that it's approximately 4" wider and longer than the quilt top. Mark the quilt top if necessary. Layer the quilt top with batting and backing, and baste the layers together. Hand or machine quilt as desired.

2. Trim the batting and backing even with the edges of the quilt top. Add a hanging sleeve if desired. Using the 2½"-wide red check bias strips, prepare the binding and sew it to the quilt.

# APRIL SHOWERS

Patterns are reversed for fusible appliqué.

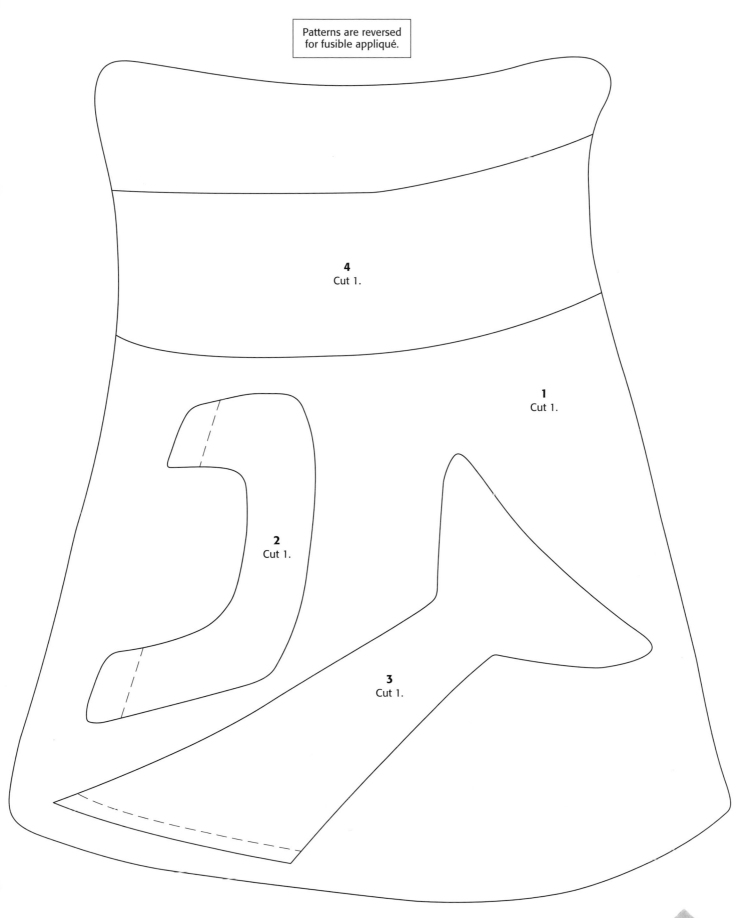

**4**
Cut 1.

**1**
Cut 1.

**2**
Cut 1.

**3**
Cut 1.

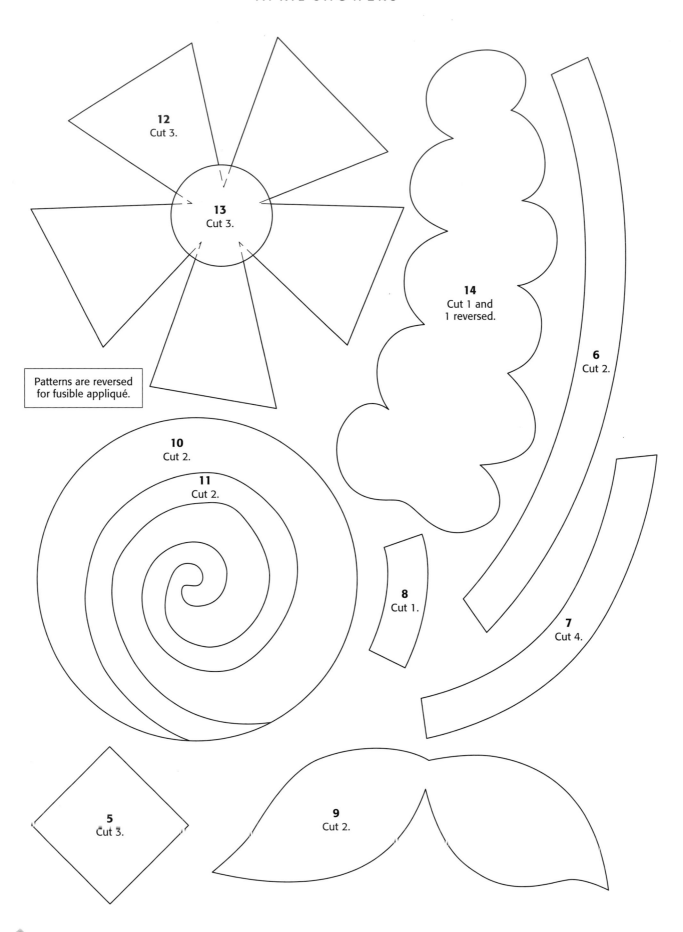

**12**
Cut 3.

**13**
Cut 3.

**14**
Cut 1 and
1 reversed.

**6**
Cut 2.

Patterns are reversed
for fusible appliqué.

**10**
Cut 2.

**11**
Cut 2.

**8**
Cut 1.

**7**
Cut 4.

**5**
Cut 3.

**9**
Cut 2.

**16**
Cut 8.

**15**
Cut 10.

# May Baskets

 o you have a round table that needs dressing up? This little topper is the perfect centerpiece. I have used simplified techniques, such as appliquéing the flower petals over a yellow square to make a detailed-looking flower, and adding buttons to the vines instead of appliquéing circles.

## Materials

*Yardage is based on 42"-wide fabric.*

⅞ yard of cream fabric for background

½ yard of green fabric for leaves and stems

⅛ yard *each* of 4 different colors for flowers

⅜ yard of brown fabric for baskets

Scrap of gold fabric for flower centers

½ yard of red stripe for binding

1 yard of fabric for backing

34" x 34" piece of batting

¾ yard of fusible web

Black pearl cotton #5

16 red buttons, ⅝" diameter

8 red buttons, ½" diameter

## Cutting

**From the green fabric, cut:**
2 strips, 3" x 42"; crosscut into 16 squares, 3" x 3"

**From the cream fabric, cut:**
1 square, 15½" x 15½"; cut twice diagonally to yield 4 triangles

1 square, 10½" x 10½"

8 squares, 5½" x 5½"

16 squares, 3" x 3"

**From the brown fabric, cut:**
3 strips, 3" x 42"; crosscut into:

    4 pieces, 3" x 10½"

    8 pieces, 3" x 5½"

**From the red stripe, cut:**
2½"-wide bias strips to total 115" in length

Quilt size: 30½" x 30½"

## Making the Blocks

1. Referring to "Folded-Corner Units" on page 7, sew a green square to a corner of each 5½" cream square. Press half the seams toward the green and half toward the cream so that the seams will nest when sewn together. Sew the units into pairs, pressing as directed by the arrow.

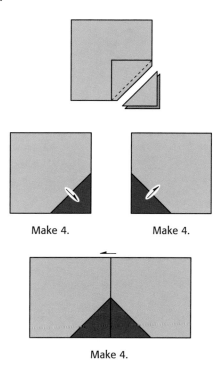

Make 4.   Make 4.

Make 4.

2. Using the folded-corner technique, sew two 3" cream squares to each 10½"-long brown piece as shown, pressing the seams as directed.

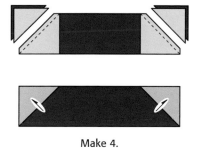

Make 4.

3. Again using the folded-corner technique, sew a 3" cream square to the left side of a 5½"-long brown piece. Sew a 3" green square to the right side. Press the seams as directed by the arrow. Make four of these units and four reverse. Sew the units into pairs, pressing as directed.

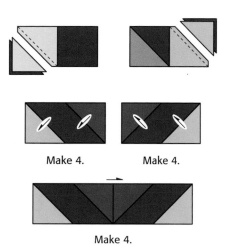

Make 4.   Make 4.

Make 4.

4. Sew the units from steps 1–3 together as shown to make four blocks. Proof each block to 10½" x 10½". Referring to "Appliqué" on page 9, prepare the appliqué shapes from the patterns on page 81. Fuse a basket handle and gold square to each block, referring to the photo on page 78 for placement. Machine appliqué these shapes using a small zigzag stitch with matching thread. Next, fuse the petals in place and blanket-stitch with black topstitching thread.

Make 4.

## Assembling the Quilt Top

1. Sew the blocks, the 10½" cream square, and the cream triangles into rows as shown, pressing the seams away from the Basket blocks. Sew the rows together and press the seams away from the center square.

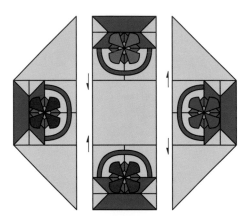

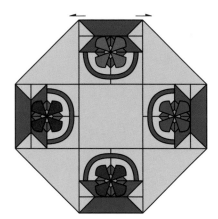

2. Fuse the stems in place and then add leaves, referring to the photo for placement. Machine appliqué using a small zigzag stitch with green thread.

## Finishing

Refer to the quilt-finishing techniques on pages 12–13, if needed.

1. Piece the quilt backing so that it's approximately 4" wider and longer than the quilt top. Mark the quilt top if necessary. Layer the quilt top with batting and backing, and baste the layers together. Hand or machine quilt as desired.

2. Trim the batting and backing even with the edges of the quilt top. Add a hanging sleeve if desired. Using the 2½"-wide red stripe bias strips, prepare the binding and sew it to the quilt.

3. Referring to the photo on page 78 for placement, use the black pearl cotton to sew the buttons along the vines.

### COLOR OPTION

I borrowed this quilt from my mom, Deb. She chose to make hers less scrappy by using one fabric for all the flowers. I like the result, and also her choice of background fabric: yellow instead of the expected cream. It really sets off the red baskets.

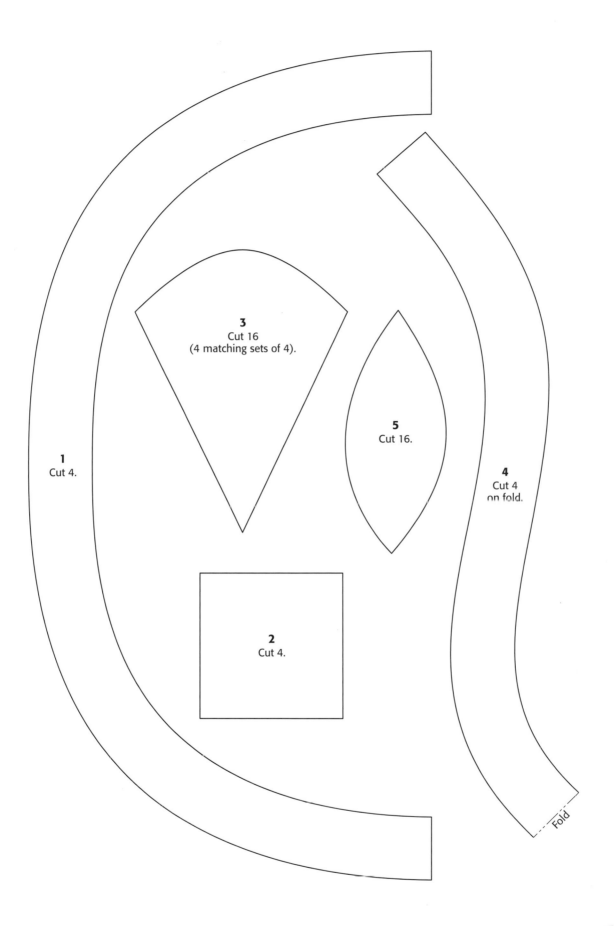

**3**
Cut 16
(4 matching sets of 4).

**5**
Cut 16.

**1**
Cut 4.

**4**
Cut 4
on fold.

**2**
Cut 4.

Fold

# Maple Harvest

I love all things that remind me of fall, and this quilt is the perfect example. It's full of movement, from the "twinkling" border to the maple leaf blocks and the appliqué. The blocks have different background colors and are arranged from light to dark, adding to the sense of movement. Notice how the appliqué shapes are stitched with a contrasting brown thread so they really pop off the black background.

## Materials

*Yardage is based on 42"-wide fabric.*

18 fat quarters in assorted colors for leaves, border, and appliqué

1⅝ yards of black fabric for dark background

1 yard of gold fabric for medium background

⅞ yard of cream fabric for light background

2 fat eighths of gold fabric for border and appliqué

2 fat eighths of black fabric for border

15" square of green plaid for flower stems

8" x 10" piece of brown fabric for basket

¾ yard of black plaid for binding

3¼ yards of fabric for backing

55" x 72" piece of batting

½ yard of fusible web

## Cutting

**From *each* of the 18 colored fabrics, cut:**
1 set* of:
    2 squares, 3⅛" x 3⅛"
    2 squares, 2¾" x 2¾"
    1 piece, 2¾" x 5"

**From the remainder of the 18 colored fabrics, cut a *total* of:**
124 squares, 3⅛" x 3⅛"

**From the cream fabric, cut:**
2 strips, 3⅛" x 42"; crosscut into 20 squares, 3⅛" x 3⅛"
1 strip, 2¾" x 42"; crosscut into 10 squares, 2¾" x 2¾"
2 strips, 2⅜" x 42"; crosscut into 20 squares, 2⅜" x 2⅜"
9 strips, 1¼" x 42"; crosscut into:
    20 pieces, 1¼" x 8¾"
    20 pieces, 1¼" x 7¼"

*\*Cut each set from 1 fabric for a consistent look within each block.*

Continued on page 84

Quilt size: 50¾" x 68"

**From the gold fabric, cut:**

1 strip, 3⅛" x 42"; crosscut into 12 squares, 3⅛" x 3⅛"

1 strip, 2⅜" x 42"; crosscut into 12 squares, 2⅜" x 2⅜"

18 strips, 1¼" x 42"; crosscut into:

    24 pieces, 1¼" x 10¼"

    36 pieces, 1¼" x 8¾"

    12 pieces, 1¼" x 7¼"

1 strip, 2¾" x 42"; crosscut into 6 squares, 2¾" x 2¾"

**From the black fabric for background, cut:**

1 strip, 8⅜" x 41¾" (piecing if needed)

3 squares, 15¼" x 15¼"; cut each square twice diagonally to yield 12 side triangles. (You will use 10.)

2 squares, 8" x 8"; cut each square once diagonally to yield 4 corner triangles

8 strips, 1¼" x 42"; crosscut into:

    12 pieces, 1¼" x 10¼"

    16 pieces, 1¼" x 8¾"

    4 pieces, 1¼" x 7¼"

4 squares, 3⅛" x 3⅛"

2 squares, 2¾" x 2¾"

4 squares, 2⅜" x 2⅜"

**From *each* of the gold fat eighths, cut:**

8 squares, 3⅛" x 3⅛" (16 total)

**From *each* of the black fat eighths, cut:**

8 squares, 3⅛" x 3⅛" (16 total)

**From the green plaid, cut:**

1¾"-wide bias strips to total 60" in length

**From the black plaid, cut:**

2½"-wide bias strips to total 250" in length

## Making the Blocks

1. From the 18 sets of colored fabrics, choose 10 sets for the light-background leaves, 6 sets for the medium-background leaves, and 2 sets for the dark-background leaves.

2. To make the 10 light-background leaves, refer to "Folded-Corner Units" on page 7 and sew a

2⅜" cream square to a 2¾" colored square as shown. Trim the outer corner to a ¼" seam allowance and press the seam toward the corner. Repeat with another 2⅜" cream square on the other side.

Make 10.

3. Referring to "Half-Square-Triangle Units" on page 7, sew 3⅛" cream and colored squares together to make 40 half-square-triangle units. Press the seams toward the colored fabric and proof each unit to 2¾" x 2¾".

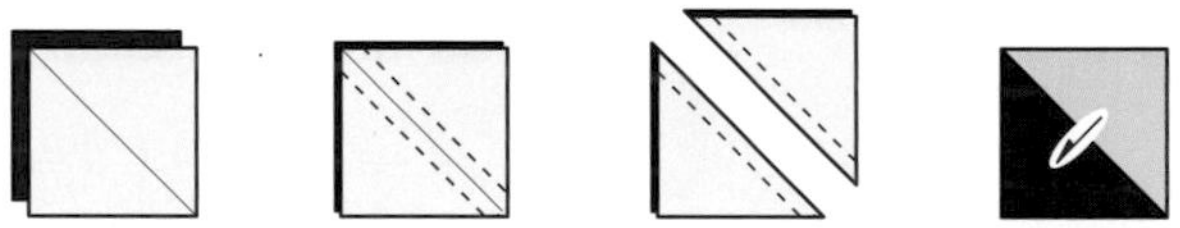

Make 4
of each fabric
(40 total).

4. Sew matching units from steps 2 and 3 together with a matching 5"-long colored piece, a matching 2¾" colored square, and a 2¾" cream square as shown. Press the seams as directed by the arrows. Proof each block to 7¼" x 7¼". Sew 7¼"-long cream pieces to opposite sides of each block and press the seams toward the strips. Repeat on the other two sides with the 8¾"-long cream pieces and press the seams toward the strips.

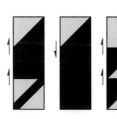 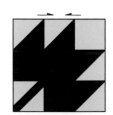

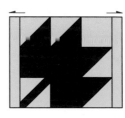 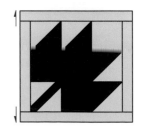

5. Border each block as in step 4 using the 8¾"-long gold pieces first and then the 10¼"-long gold strips. Proof each block to 10¼" x 10¼".

Make 10.

6. To make the six medium-background blocks, repeat steps 2–5, using a *gold* background first border and a *black* final border.

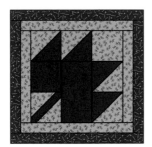

Make 6.

7. To make the two dark-background blocks, repeat steps 2–5, using a *black* background first border and a *gold* final border.

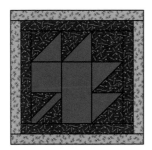

Make 2.

## Assembling the Quilt Top

1. Lay out the blocks and the side and corner triangles as shown. Sew the blocks into rows, pressing the seams toward the black. Sew the rows together, pressing the seams in either direction. Add the corner triangles and press the seams toward the black. Proof the quilt-top center to 41¾" x 55⅝".

2. To make the stems for the appliqué design, sew the green plaid bias strips together end to end and press the strip in half lengthwise, wrong sides together. Press in half again, but center the raw edge in the back of the strip.

3. Referring to "Appliqué" on page 9, prepare the appliqué shapes from the patterns on page 87. Lay the 8⅜"-wide black strip next to the bottom of the quilt, but don't sew it on yet. Position the appliqué shapes and stems on the strip, referring to the photo on page 83. Machine appliqué the shapes onto the border, leaving off the ones that will overlap onto the quilt-top center. I used a small zigzag stitch with monofilament thread to attach the stems. The orange flower centers were appliquéd using a small zigzag stitch with matching thread. All the other shapes were appliquéd using a

blanket stitch with brown topstitching thread. Referring to "Adding the Borders" on page 8 as needed, sew the border to the bottom of the quilt-top center, and appliqué the remaining shapes that overlap onto the center.

4. Referring to "Half-Square-Triangle Units" on page 7, use the remaining 3⅛" colored, gold, and black squares to make 156 half-square-triangle units.

5. Sew the border units from step 4 together as shown to make the three border strips. Use 56 units for each side-border strip and proof to a length of 63½". Use 44 units for the top-border strip and proof to a length of 50½". Press the seams in one direction or open to reduce bulk.

Side border.
Make 2.

Top border.
Make 1.

6. Sew the side-border strips to the quilt top and press the seams toward the black. Sew the top-border strip to the quilt top and press the seams toward the black.

## Finishing

Refer to the quilt-finishing techniques on pages 12–13, if needed.

1. Piece the quilt backing so that it's approximately 4" wider and longer than the quilt top. Mark the quilt top if necessary. Layer the quilt top with batting and backing, and baste the layers together. Hand or machine quilt as desired.

2. Trim the batting and backing even with the edges of the quilt top. Add a hanging sleeve if desired. Using the 2½"-wide black plaid bias strips, prepare the binding and sew it to the quilt.

## HOOKED-RUG OPTION

I couldn't envision this quilt in anything too different from the original colors, but I could envision taking the appliqué design and turning it into a hooked rug. When you think about that, any appliqué design could be a pattern for a rug!

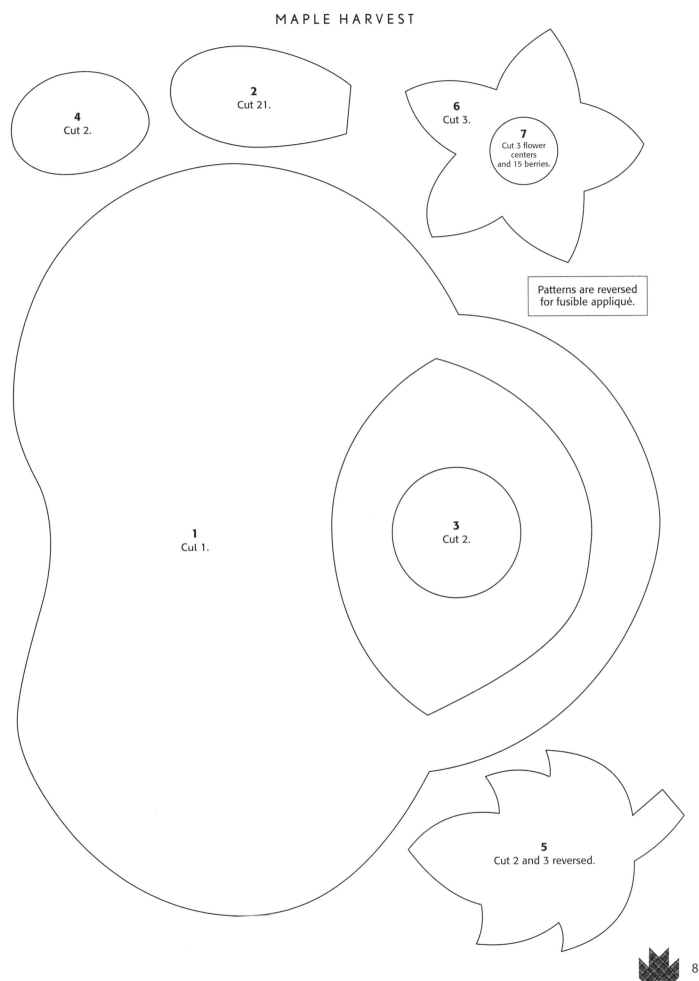

**4**
Cut 2.

**2**
Cut 21.

**6**
Cut 3.

**7**
Cut 3 flower
centers
and 15 berries.

Patterns are reversed
for fusible appliqué.

**1**
Cut 1.

**3**
Cut 2.

**5**
Cut 2 and 3 reversed.

# Sunny Morning

The pieced pattern of this quilt reminds me of a mosaic floor, with an inlaid design in the center. Simple Nine Patch and Snowball blocks create this wonderful pattern. The floral border softens the quilt and pulls everything together.

## Materials

*Yardage is based on 42"-wide fabric.*

1 yard of blue print for Nine Patch and Snowball blocks

⅞ yard of cream check for snowball blocks

¾ yard of yellow floral for outer border

¾ yard of red fabric for setting triangles and appliqué

⅝ yard of yellow fabric for Nine Patch blocks

Scraps of green and pink for appliqué

½ yard of green fabric for binding

2⅞ yards of fabric for backing

50" x 50" piece of batting

⅓ yard of fusible web

## Cutting

**From the blue print, cut:**

11 strips, 2¼" x 42"; crosscut *3 strips* into 48 squares, 2¼" x 2¼"

4 squares, 3½" x 3½"

**From the yellow fabric, cut:**

7 strips, 2¼" x 42"

**From the cream check, cut:**

1 square, 14¼" x 14¼"

12 squares, 5¾" x 5¾"

**From the red fabric, cut:**

4 squares, 8¾" x 8¾"; cut each square twice diagonally to yield 16 side triangles

2 squares, 4⅝" x 4⅝"; cut each square once diagonally to yield 4 corner triangles

2 strips, 1½" x 42"; crosscut into:

  2 strips, 1½" x 16¼"

  2 strips, 1½" x 14¼"

**From the yellow floral, cut:**

5 strips, 4½" x 42"

**From the green fabric, cut:**

5 strips, 2½" x 42"

Quilt size: 45⅝" x 45⅝"

## Making the Blocks

1. Sew two of the blue print strips and one yellow strip together as shown, pressing the seams toward the blue. Make three of these strip sets. Cut into 40 segments, 2¼" wide. Sew two of the remaining yellow strips and one blue print strip together as shown, pressing the seams toward the blue. Make two of these strip sets. Cut into 20 segments, 2¼" wide.

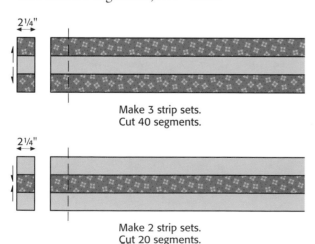

Make 3 strip sets.
Cut 40 segments.

Make 2 strip sets.
Cut 20 segments.

2. Sew the segments from step 1 together as shown to make 20 Nine Patch blocks. Press the seams as directed and proof each block to 5¾" x 5¾".

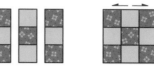

Make 20.

3. Referring to "Folded-Corner Units" on page 7, sew the 2¼" blue print squares to the 5¾" cream check squares. Press the seams toward the blue and proof each block to 5¾" x 5¾".

Make 12.

4. Use the folded-corner technique to sew the 3½" blue print squares to the 14¼" cream check square. Press the seams toward the blue. Frame the block with the red 1½" strips by first sewing the 14¼"-long strips to opposite sides, and then sewing the 16¼"-long strips to the remaining two sides. Press the seams toward the red.

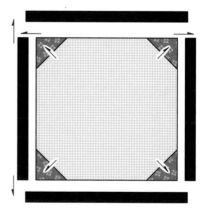

5. Referring to "Appliqué" on page 9, prepare the appliqué shapes from the patterns on page 91. Fuse the shapes to the center square, referring to the photo above left for placement. Machine appliqué using a blanket stitch with matching threads.

## Assembling the Quilt Top

1. Lay out the Nine Patch blocks, the Snowball blocks, the center block, and the side and corner triangles as shown. Sew the blocks and side triangles into rows, pressing the seams toward the Nine Patch blocks. Sew the rows together, pressing the seams in either direction. Add the corner triangles and press the seams toward the triangles. Proof the quilt-top center to 37⅝" x 37⅝", leaving ¼" seam allowance beyond all block points.

2. Referring to "Adding the Borders" on page 8 as needed, cut off two yellow floral strips to a length of 37⅝". Sew them to the sides of the quilt-top center and press the seams toward the border. Sew the remaining yellow floral strips together end to end and cut off two lengths at 45⅝". Sew these to the top and bottom of the quilt, pressing the seams toward the border.

## Finishing

Refer to the quilt-finishing techniques on pages 12–13, if needed.

1. Piece the quilt backing so that it's approximately 4" wider and longer than the quilt top. Mark the quilt top if necessary. Layer the quilt top with batting and backing, and baste the layers together. Hand or machine quilt as desired.

2. Trim the batting and backing even with the edges of the quilt top. Add a hanging sleeve if desired. Using the 2½"-wide green strips, prepare the binding and sew it to the quilt.

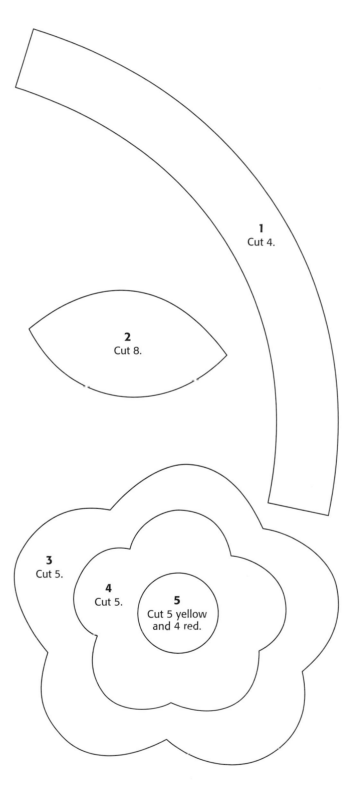

**1**
Cut 4.

**2**
Cut 8.

**3**
Cut 5.

**4**
Cut 5.

**5**
Cut 5 yellow
and 4 red.

# Arbor Rose

**G**reat movement and color are the key to this stunning quilt. You will piece the quilt top in four sections that are appliquéd separately for easier handling.

## Materials

*Yardage is based on 42"-wide fabric.*

1⅝ yards of cream fabric for blocks

1¼ yards of tan fabric for blocks

1 yard of red fabric for outer border

⅞ yard of yellow print for blocks

⅞ yard of purple fabric for inner border and flower centers

⅝ yard of green fabric for stems and leaves

¼ yard *each* of 2 red prints for roses

⅛ yard of yellow for flower centers

⅛ yard of black for flower centers

⅝ yard of black plaid for binding

4 yards of fabric for backing

68" x 68" piece of batting

2 yards of fusible web

## Cutting

**From the cream fabric, cut:**

8 strips, 4⅜" x 42"; crosscut into 72 squares, 4⅜" x 4⅜"

8 strips, 2" x 42"; crosscut into 72 pieces, 2" x 4"

**From the tan fabric, cut:**

4 strips, 4⅜" x 42"; crosscut into 36 squares, 4⅜" x 4⅜"

9 strips, 2" x 42"; crosscut into:

　72 pieces, 2" x 4"

　18 squares, 2" x 2"

**From the yellow print, cut:**

4 strips, 4⅜" x 42"; crosscut into 36 squares, 4⅜" x 4⅜"

1 strip, 2" x 42"; crosscut into 18 squares, 2" x 2"

4 squares, 5" x 5"

**From the purple fabric, cut:**

6 strips, 2¼" x 42"

**From the red fabric, cut:**

6 strips, 5" x 42"

**From the green fabric, cut:**

2"-wide bias strips to total 290" in length (cut from the center of the yardage)

**From the black plaid, cut:**

2½"-wide bias strips to total 270" in length

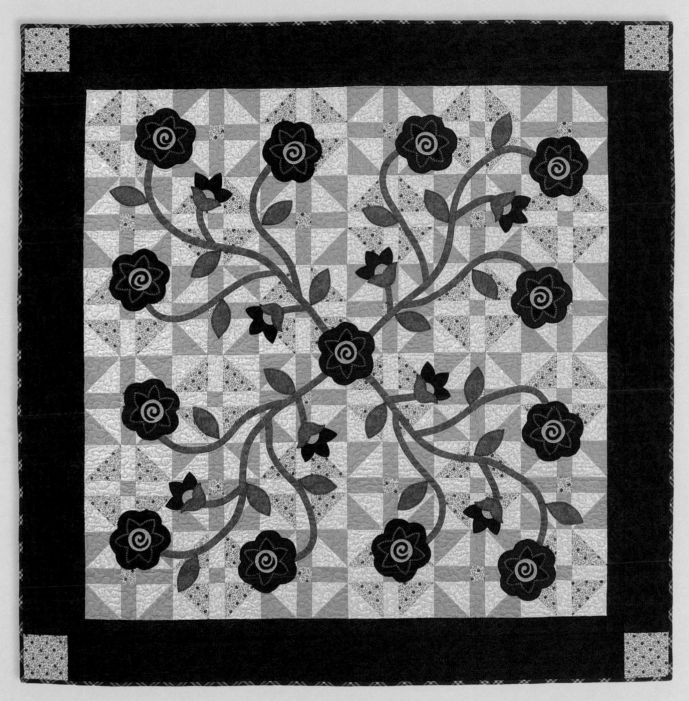

Quilt size: 64" x 64"

Designed by Deb Mulder and Heather Mulder Peterson

## Making the Blocks

1. Referring to "Half-Square-Triangle Units" on page 7, sew 36 of the 4⅜" cream squares together with the 4⅜" tan squares to make 72 half-square-triangle units. Press the seams toward the tan and proof each unit to 4" x 4".

2. Using the half-square-triangle technique, sew the 36 remaining cream squares together with the 4⅜" yellow print squares to make 72 half-square-triangle units. Press the seams toward the tan and proof each unit to 4" x 4".

3. Sew the cream-and-tan units from step 1 together with the 2" x 4" tan pieces and the 2" yellow print squares as shown to make 18 blocks. Press all the seams toward the tan rectangles. Proof each block to 9" x 9".

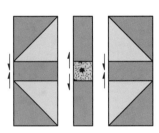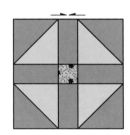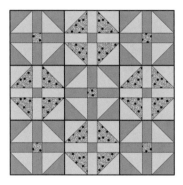

Make 18.

4. Sew the cream-and-yellow print units from step 2 together with the 2" x 4" cream pieces and the 2" tan squares as shown to make 18 blocks. Press all the seams away from the cream rectangles. Proof each block to 9" x 9".

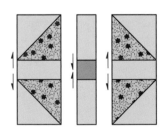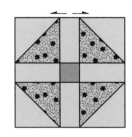

Make 18.

## Assembling the Quilt Top

1. Sew the blocks into four sections as shown, making two sections of each block arrangement. Proof each section to 26" x 26".

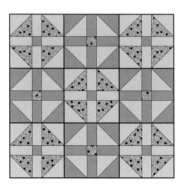

Make 2.

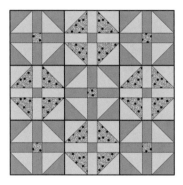

Make 2.

2. Sew the 2"-wide green bias strips together end to end, on the diagonal, and press the strip in half with wrong sides together. Fold the strip again, centering the raw edge in the back of the strip; press. Position the strips on the sections from step 1, referring to the photo on page 93 for placement. Machine appliqué the vines using a small zigzag stitch with matching thread.

3. Referring to "Appliqué" on page 9, prepare the appliqué shapes from the patterns on page 96. Be sure to trim out the center of the fusible material on the larger shapes. First, machine appliqué the black swirl to the yellow flower center using a small zigzag stitch with matching thread. Next, add the yellow flower center to the purple flower center using a small zigzag stitch with matching thread. You can trim the layers of fabric behind the shapes as you go, to

help reduce the bulk. Add the purple flower center to the red flower and machine appliqué using a blanket stitch with black topstitching thread. Position the appliqué shapes (except the center flower) onto the block sections. Appliqué using a blanket stitch with black topstitching thread on all the shapes except the yellow flower center on the flower bud. I used a zigzag stitch with matching thread for this shape. You will add the center flower after step 7.

4. Sew all four block sections together as shown in the photo and proof the quilt-top center to 51½" x 51½".

5. Referring to "Adding the Borders" on page 8 as needed, sew the purple strips together end to end. Cut off two lengths at 51½" and sew them to the sides of the quilt-top center. Cut off two lengths at 55" and sew these to the top and bottom of the quilt top. Press all the seams toward the purple.

6. Sew the red strips together end to end and cut off four lengths at 55". Sew two of these strips to the sides of the quilt top. Sew the 5" yellow print squares to the ends of the remaining red strips, pressing the seams toward the yellow. Sew these strips to the top and bottom of the quilt top. Press all the seams toward the purple.

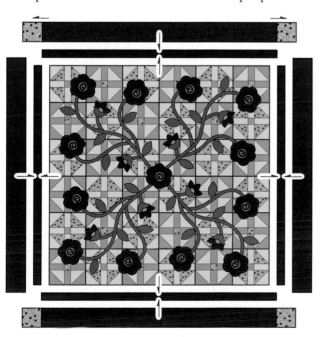

## Finishing

Refer to the quilt-finishing techniques on pages 12–13, if needed.

1. Piece the quilt backing so that it's approximately 4" wider and longer than the quilt top. Mark the quilt top if necessary. Layer the quilt top with batting and backing, and baste the layers together. Hand or machine quilt as desired.

2. Trim the batting and backing even with the edges of the quilt top. Add a hanging sleeve if desired. Using the 2½"-wide black plaid bias strips, prepare the binding and sew it to the quilt.

## COLOR OPTION

I made this quilt more primitive-looking by using a black background and wool appliqué. I also did it on a smaller scale, making only nine blocks and turning it into a "European-size" pillow. The appliqué shapes are the same as on the original quilt; they are just arranged differently.

Patterns are reversed
for fusible appliqué.

**2**
Cut 13.

**1**
Cut 13.

**3**
Cut 13.

**4**
Cut 13.

**5**
Cut 8.

**6**
Cut 8.

**8**
Cut 20.

**7**
Cut 8.

# Snails in the Sand

My first trip to the ocean inspired this cheery quilt. I was obviously impressed by the huge ocean waves, and they became the focal point of this design. I added a few of my favorite flowers and a "sandy" border.

## Materials

*Yardage is based on 42"-wide fabric.*

½ yard *each* of 7 different cream prints for blocks

7 fat quarters of different blue prints for blocks

1¾ yards of yellow print for outer border and appliqué

1⅓ yards of blue plaid for alternate blocks

¼ yard *each* of green and blue check for appliqué

⅝ yard of blue check for binding

4 yards of backing fabric

67" x 67" piece of batting

## Cutting

*Lay out the blue and cream triangles from smallest to largest and sew them to each block in that order (see step 2 of "Making the Blocks").*

**From the cream prints, cut a *total* of:**

46 squares, 5½" x 5½"

7 squares, 6¼" x 6¼"; cut each square twice diagonally to yield 28 triangles. (You will use 26.)

13 squares, 5⅞" x 5⅞"; cut each square once diagonally to yield 26 triangles

7 squares, 3¾" x 3¾"; cut each square twice diagonally to yield 28 triangles. (You will use 26.)

13 squares, 3⅜" x 3⅜"; cut each square once diagonally to yield 26 triangles

4 strips, 1¾" x 14"

**From the blue prints, cut a *total* of:**

7 squares, 6¼" x 6¼"; cut each square twice diagonally to yield 28 triangles. (You will use 26.)

13 squares, 5⅞" x 5⅞"; cut each square once diagonally to yield 26 triangles

7 squares, 3¾" x 3¾"; cut each square twice diagonally to yield 28 triangles. (You will use 26.)

13 squares, 3⅜" x 3⅜"; cut each square once diagonally to yield 26 triangles

4 strips, 1¾" x 14"

**From the blue plaid, cut:**

4 strips, 10½" x 42"; crosscut into 12 squares, 10½" x 10½"

**From the yellow print, cut:**

8 strips, 7" x 42"; crosscut into:

   8 pieces, 7" x 20½"

   2 pieces, 7" x 17"

   2 pieces, 7" x 10½"

   2 squares, 7" x 7"

**From the blue check, cut:**

2½"-wide bias strips to total 270" in length

## Making the Blocks

1. Sew the 1¾" cream strips and blue strips together along their long edges to make four strip sets. Press the seams toward the blue. Cut into 26 segments, 1¾" wide. Sew the segments together as shown to make 13 four-patch units. Proof each unit to 3" x 3".

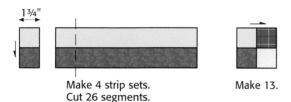

Make 4 strip sets.
Cut 26 segments.                    Make 13.

2. Sew two of the smallest blue triangles to opposite sides of each four-patch unit. Press the seams away from the center. Repeat on the remaining sides using the smallest cream triangles. Continue adding blue and cream triangles to the block as shown. Make 13 Snails Trail blocks and proof each block to 10½" x 10½".

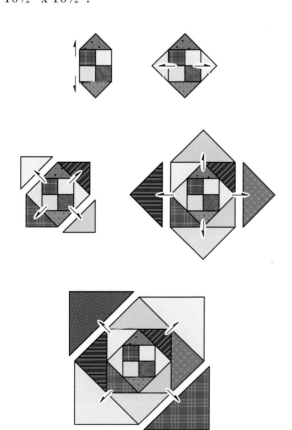

Make 13.

3. Referring to "Folded-Corner Units" on page 7, sew two 5½" cream squares to each blue plaid square as shown. Press the seams toward the blue plaid.

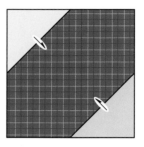

Make 12.

4. Referring to "Appliqué" on page 9, prepare the appliqué shapes from the patterns on page 101. Fuse the shapes to six of the blocks made in step 3, referring to the photo on page 98 for placement. Machine appliqué using a small zigzag stitch with monofilament or nylon thread on top and regular thread in the bobbin (loosen the top tension if necessary).

## Assembling the Quilt Top

1. Sew the blocks into five rows of five blocks each, referring to the photo for placement of the appliqué blocks. Press the seams away from the Snails Trail blocks. Sew the rows together and press the seams in either direction. Proof the quilt-top center to 50½" x 50½".

2. Using the folded-corner technique, sew the remaining 5½" cream squares to the yellow print pieces as shown. Press the seams toward the yellow.

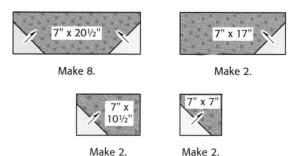

7" x 20½"                    7" x 17"

Make 8.                      Make 2.

7" x 10½"        7" x 7"

Make 2.          Make 2.

3. Using the pieces from step 2, sew two 20½" pieces and one 10½" piece together to make two strips for the side borders. Sew two 20½" pieces, one 17" piece, and one 7" square together to make strips for the top and bottom borders.

4. Referring to "Adding the Borders" on page 8 as needed, sew the side borders to the quilt-top center, and press the seams toward the borders. Sew the top and bottom borders to the quilt top, pressing the seams toward the borders.

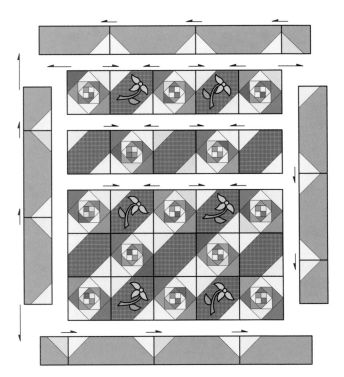

## Finishing

Refer to the quilt-finishing techniques on pages 12–13, if needed.

1. Piece the quilt backing so that it's approximately 4" wider and longer than the quilt top. Mark the quilt top if necessary. Layer the quilt top with batting and backing, and baste the layers together. Hand or machine quilt as desired.

2. Trim the batting and backing even with the edges of the quilt top. Add a hanging sleeve if desired. Using the 2½"-wide blue check bias strips, prepare the binding and sew it to the quilt.

Quilt size: 63½" x 63½"

## COLOR OPTION

I love how different this quilt looks from the original. I chose red and black for my blocks and borrowed the appliqué shapes from "Christmas Glow" on page 63, enlarging the images by 140%.

Patterns are reversed for fusible appliqué.

**4**
Cut 6.

**2**
Cut 3 and 3 reversed for leaves.

**1**
Cut 3 and 3 reversed.

**2**
Cut 9 and 9 reversed for petals.

# Katie's Cottage Tablecloth

$\mathcal{I}$ love the simplicity of this quilt. There is no fussy piecing and just a touch of cheery appliqué. It looks great spread out diagonally on a large table.

## Materials

*Yardage is based on 42"-wide fabric.*

1 yard of red floral for quilt center and outer border

1 yard of black fabric for appliquéd border

⅓ yard of green fabric for sashing and leaves

Fat quarter of black floral for center

⅛ yard *each* of red dot and red check fabrics for flowers

⅛ yard of yellow fabric for posts and flower centers

½ yard of red check for binding

2⅞ yards of fabric for backing

49" x 49" piece of batting

½ yard of fusible material

## Cutting

**From the black floral, cut:**
1 square, 11½" x 11½"

**From the red floral, cut:**
2 strips, 8½" x 42"; crosscut *each strip* into 2 rectangles, 8½" x 11½", and 2 squares, 8½" x 8½" (4 rectangles and 4 squares total)

5 strips, 3" x 42"

**From the yellow fabric, cut:**
1 strip, 1½" x 14"

4 squares, 1½" x 1½"

**From the green fabric, cut:**
4 strips, 1½" x 42"; crosscut into:

4 pieces, 1½" x 11½"

8 pieces, 1½" x 8½"

1 strip, 1½" x 26"

1 strip, 1½" x 14"

**From the black fabric, cut:**
4 strips, 5½" x 42"; crosscut into:

4 pieces, 5½" x 12½"

4 pieces, 5½" x 9½"

4 pieces, 5½" x 7½"

1 strip, 4½" x 26"

1 strip, 3½" x 14"

**From the red check, cut:**
2½"-wide bias strips to total 190" in length

## Assembling the Quilt Top

1. Lay out the black floral square, the four red floral rectangles, the four red floral squares, the four yellow squares, and the 11½"-long and 8½"-long green pieces as shown. Sew the pieces into rows, pressing all the seams

Quilt size: 44½" x 44½"

toward the green. Sew the rows together, pressing the seams toward the green, and proof the quilt-top center to 29½" x 29½".

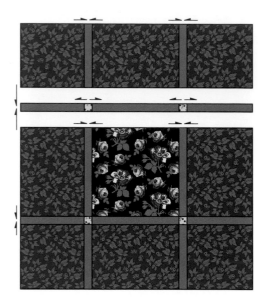

2. Sew the 4½" x 26" black strip and the 26"-long green strip together, pressing the seam toward the green. Cut into 16 segments, 1½" wide.

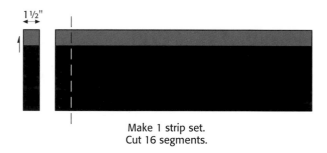

1½"

Make 1 strip set.
Cut 16 segments.

3. Sew the 3½" x 14" black strip, the 14"-long green strip, and the 14"-long yellow strip together as shown, pressing the seams toward the green. Cut into eight segments, 1½" wide.

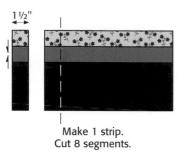

1½"

Make 1 strip.
Cut 8 segments.

4. Sew the segments from steps 2 and 3 together as shown to make eight border units.

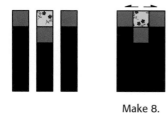

Make 8.

5. Sew the border units and the 5½"-wide black pieces into border strips as shown, being careful to sew the black pieces of the correct size in the correct place.

6. Referring to "Adding the Borders" on page 8 as needed, sew the two shorter border strips to the sides of the quilt-top center, and sew the two longer border strips to the top and bottom. Press all seams toward the borders. Proof the quilt top to 39½" x 39½".

7. Cut two of the 3" red strips to a length of 39½", and sew them to the sides of the quilt top. Cut two more lengths to 44½" (piecing as needed), and sew these to the top and bottom of the quilt top. Press all seams toward the red borders.

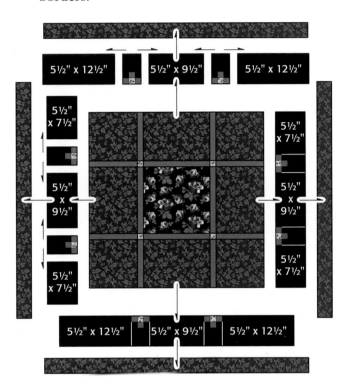

8. Referring to "Appliqué" on page 9, prepare the appliqué shapes from the patterns below. Fuse the shapes in place, referring to the photo on page 103 for placement. Machine appliqué the flowers using a blanket stitch with black topstitching thread. Use a small zigzag stitch with matching thread for the leaves and flower centers.

## Finishing

Refer to the quilt-finishing techniques on pages 12–13, if needed.

1. Piece the quilt backing so that it's approximately 4" wider and longer than the quilt top. Mark the quilt top if necessary. Layer the quilt top with batting and backing, and baste the layers together. Hand or machine quilt as desired.

2. Trim the batting and backing even with the edges of the quilt top. Add a hanging sleeve if desired. Using the 2½"-wide red check strips, prepare the binding and sew it to the quilt.

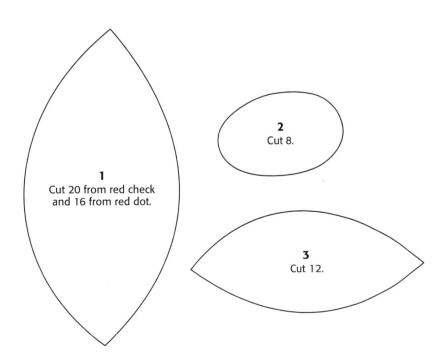

**1**
Cut 20 from red check
and 16 from red dot.

**2**
Cut 8.

**3**
Cut 12.

# Peggy's Posies

**A**nything plaid is a favorite of mine, and this quilt uses fabric pieced to look like a plaid. Follow the pressing instructions and everything will nest together easily. The simple appliqué shapes soften the strong lines of the pieced top.

## Materials

*Yardage is based on 42"-wide fabric.*

1⅛ yards of yellow print for Flower blocks and setting triangles

⅞ yard of black plaid for outer border

⅞ yard of red plaid for Nine Patch blocks

⅔ yard of red fabric for outer border and appliqué

⅓ yard of black print for Nine Patch blocks

⅓ yard of green fabric for Flower blocks

⅝ yard of green fabric for binding

3 yards of fabric for backing

50" x 62" piece of batting

¼ yard of fusible web

## Cutting

**From the red plaid, cut:**
6 strips, 4" x 42"

**From the black print, cut:**
3 strips, 1½" x 42"
1 strip, 4" x 42"; crosscut into 2 pieces, 4" x 20"
1 piece, 1½" x 12"

**From the green fabric, cut**
2 strips, 1½" x 28"
1 piece, 1½" x 20"
2 pieces, 4" x 12"

**From the yellow print, cut:**
4 strips, 4" x 28"
1 square, 9¼" x 9¼"
5 squares, 8⅞" x 8⅞"

**From the red fabric, cut:**
1 square, 9¼" x 9¼"
7 squares, 8⅞" x 8⅞"

**From the black plaid, cut:**
4 squares, 12⅝" x 12⅝"; cut each square twice diagonally to yield 16 side triangles. (You will use 14.)
2 squares, 6⅝" x 6⅝"; cut each square once diagonally to yield 4 corner triangles

**From the green binding fabric, cut:**
6 strips, 2½" x 42"

Quilt size: 45¾" x 57"

## Making the Blocks

1. Sew the red plaid strips and the 42"-long black print strips together along their long edges as shown to make three strip sets. Press the seams toward the black. Cut into 24 segments, 4" wide.

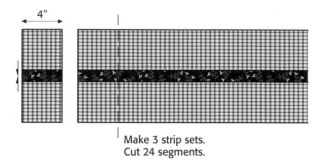

Make 3 strip sets.
Cut 24 segments.

2. Sew the two 4" x 20" black pieces and the 1½" x 20" green piece together as shown to make one strip set. Press the seams toward the black. Cut into 12 segments, 1½" wide.

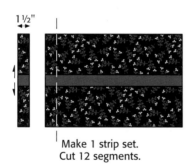

Make 1 strip set.
Cut 12 segments.

3. Sew the 4" x 28" yellow print strips and the 1½" x 28" green strips together as shown to make two strip sets. Press the seams toward the yellow. Cut into 12 segments, 4" wide.

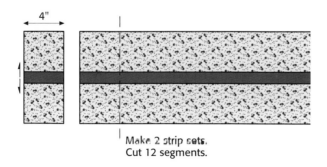

Make 2 strip sets.
Cut 12 segments.

4. Sew the 4" x 12" green strips and the 1½" x 12" black strip together as shown to make one strip set. Press the seams toward the black. Cut into six segments, 1½" wide.

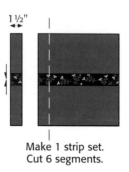

Make 1 strip set.
Cut 6 segments.

5. Sew the red-and-black segments from step 1 together with the black-and-green segments from step 2 as shown. Press the seams as directed by the arrows. Proof each block to 8½" x 8½".

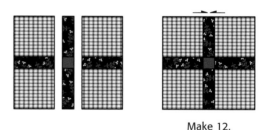

Make 12.

6. Sew the yellow-and-green segments from step 3 together with the green-and-black segments from step 4 as shown. Press the seams as directed by the arrows. Proof each block to 8½" x 8½".

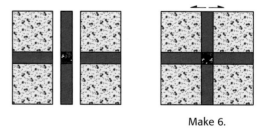

Make 6.

7. Referring to "Appliqué" on page 9, prepare the appliqué shapes from the pattern on page 109. Fuse the shapes in place, referring to the photo on page 107 for placement. Machine appliqué the petals using a blanket stitch with black topstitching thread.

8. Referring to "Half-Square-Triangle Units" on page 7, sew the 8⅞" yellow print squares and five of the 8⅞" red squares together to make 10 half-square-triangle blocks. Press the seams toward the red and proof each block to 8½" x 8½".

9. Using the half-square-triangle technique, sew the 9¼" squares of yellow print and red fabric together to make two half-square-triangle units. Pair these units with the two remaining 8⅞" red squares, right sides together. Draw a diagonal line in the direction shown across the wrong side of the pieced unit. Sew ¼" from both sides of the line and cut on the line. Press the seams toward the large red triangle and proof each corner block to 8½" x 8½".

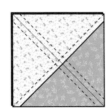
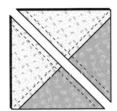

Make 2 of each.

## Assembling the Quilt Top

Lay out the Flower blocks, the Nine Patch blocks, the half-square-triangle blocks, the corner blocks, and the side and corner triangles as shown. Sew the blocks and side triangles into rows, pressing the seams away from the Flower blocks and half-square-triangle blocks. Sew the rows together, pressing the seams in either direction. Add the corner triangles and press the seams toward the triangles.

## Finishing

Refer to the quilt-finishing techniques on pages 12–13, if needed.

1. Piece the quilt backing so that it's approximately 4" wider and longer than the quilt top. Mark the quilt top if necessary. Layer the quilt top with batting and backing, and baste the layers together. Hand or machine quilt as desired.

2. Trim the batting and backing even with the edges of the quilt top. Add a hanging sleeve if desired. Using the 2½"-wide green strips, prepare the binding and sew it to the quilt.

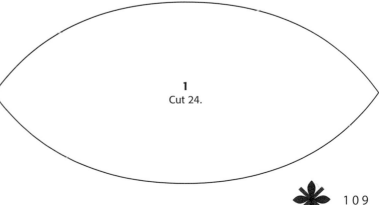

1
Cut 24.

109

# Scraps and Strips

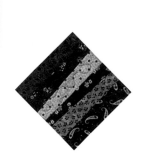

Do you have a stash of assorted leftover strips? The block in this quilt begins with a muslin foundation, and you use strips of any size to sew and flip until it's covered—you don't even have to worry about your seam allowance or sewing straight. When you are done, you just square it up to the right size. There is also a simple technique used for piecing the borders. The result is a floating pattern that looks like confetti pieces lying around the quilt.

## Materials

*Yardage is based on 42"-wide fabric.*

11 fat quarters *or* 2¾ yards *total* of assorted colors for blocks and pieced borders

1⅓ yards of muslin for block foundation

1⅓ yards of burgundy fabric for outer border

1⅛ yards of black fabric for sashing and inner border

⅛ yard of gold fabric for posts

¾ yard of black plaid for binding

3¼ yards of fabric for backing

55" x 64" piece of batting

## Cutting

**From the assorted colored fabrics, cut a *total* of:**
130 pieces, from 1¾" to 2¼" wide x 8¾" long
100 pieces, 2⅛" x 3¾"

**From the muslin, cut:**
5 strips, 8½" x 42"; crosscut into 20 squares, 8½" x 8½"

**From the black fabric, cut:**
7 strips, 1⅛" x 42"; crosscut into 31 pieces, 1⅛" x 8"

6 strips, 2⅛" x 42"; crosscut into 104 squares, 2⅛" x 2⅛"

2 strips, 3" x 42"

2 strips, 2½" x 42"

**From the gold fabric, cut:**
12 squares, 1⅛" x 1⅛"

**From the burgundy fabric, cut:**
6 strips, 4½" x 42"

6 strips, 2⅛" x 42"; crosscut into 100 squares, 2⅛" x 2⅛"

4 squares, 3¾" x 3¾"

**From the black plaid, cut:**
2½"-wide bias strips to total 230" in length

Quilt size: 50⅞" x 60"

## Making the Blocks

Lay one of the colored strips right side up on a muslin foundation block. Lay another colored strip right side down on the first strip and sew. Before pressing, trim the seam allowance to ¼" if needed to help reduce bulk. Press the seam as directed by the arrow. Lay another colored strip right side down, angling if desired but watching to see that the strip below will be caught in the seam allowance. Sew and press. Continue across the block as shown and then trim the block to 8" x 8". Make 20 of these strip-pieced blocks.

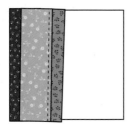
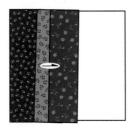

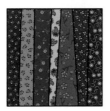

Make 20.

## Assembling the Quilt Top

1. Sew the blocks together with the 1⅛" x 8" black strips and the 1⅛" gold squares as shown. Press the seams toward the black sashing strips. Proof the quilt-top center to 32⅜" x 40½".

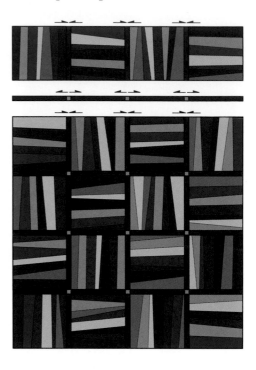

2. Referring to "Adding the Borders" on page 8 as needed, cut the 2½"-wide black strips to a length of 40½" (piecing as needed) and sew them to the sides of the quilt-top center, pressing the seams toward the black. Cut the 3"-wide black strips to a length of 36⅜" and sew these to the top and bottom of the quilt top, pressing the seams toward the black. Proof the quilt top to 36⅜" x 45½".

3. Referring to "Folded-Corner Units" on page 7, sew a 2⅛" black square to a 3¾" burgundy square as shown. Make four of these corner units and set them aside for step 5.

Make 4.

4. Sew the 2⅛" x 3¾" colored pieces into pairs, pressing the seams open. Using the folded-corner technique, sew the 2⅛" black squares and burgundy squares to each unit as shown. Be careful that the center seam is between the black and burgundy triangles. Press the seams toward the triangles.

5. Sew the step 4 units into two rows of 14 units each and proof each row to a length of 45½". Press the seams open to reduce bulk. Sew the strips to the sides of the quilt top as shown and press the seams toward the black borders. Sew the remaining units into two rows of 11 units each and proof each row to a length of 36¼". Sew the corner units from step 3 to the ends of each row, and then sew them to the top and bottom of the quilt top, pressing the seams toward the black borders. Proof the quilt top to 42¾" x 52".

Side pieced border.
Make 2.

Top/bottom pieced border.
Make 2.

6. Sew the burgundy strips together end to end. Cut off two lengths at 52" and sew them to the sides of the quilt top. Press the seams toward the outer border. Cut off two lengths at 50¾" and sew these to the top and bottom of the quilt top. Press the seams toward the outer border.

## Finishing

Refer to the quilt-finishing techniques on pages 12–13, if needed.

1. Piece the quilt backing so that it's approximately 4" wider and longer than the quilt top. Mark the quilt top if necessary. Layer the quilt top with batting and backing, and baste the layers together. Hand or machine quilt as desired.

2. Trim the batting and backing even with the edges of the quilt top. Add a hanging sleeve if desired. Using the 2½"-wide black plaid bias strips, prepare the binding and sew it to the quilt.

# Midnight Garden

ip into your stash of scraps for this quilt. Any size scrap can be used to make the Crazy Quilt blocks. Save your smaller sizes for the appliquéd "tongue" border and the larger sizes for the outer pieced border. It looks like it has difficult set-in black triangles, but these are simply made from half-square triangles with added black folded corners. When you put them together, this great border is the result.

## Materials

*Yardage is based on 42"-wide fabric.*

16 fat quarters *or* 4 yards *total* of assorted colors for pieced blocks, borders, and appliqué

3⅛ yards of black solid for appliqué blocks and borders

1¾ yards of muslin for Crazy Quilt block foundations

1⅜ yards of red print for borders

1½ yards of black plaid for borders

1 fat quarter of black print for Crazy Quilt blocks

1 fat quarter of green fabric for appliqué

⅞ yard of green plaid for binding

8¼ yards of fabric for backing

98" x 98" piece of batting

2 yards of fusible web

## Cutting

**From the muslin, cut:**
5 strips, 11" x 42"; crosscut into 13 squares, 11" x 11"

**From the assorted colors, cut a *total* of:**
56 squares, 6¾" x 6¾" (for outer pieced border)

**From the black solid, cut:**
4 strips, 10½" x 42"; crosscut into 12 squares, 10½" x 10½"

6 strips, 6½" x 42"; crosscut *1 strip* into 4 squares, 6½" x 6½"

7 strips, 2¼" x 42"; crosscut into 112 squares, 2¼" x 2¼"

**From the red print, cut:**
7 strips, 5½" x 42"

**From the black plaid, cut:**
17 strips, 2¾" x 42"

**From the green plaid, cut:**
10 strips, 2½" x 42"

Quilt size: 93¼" x 93¼"

## Making the Blocks

Cut the fabrics to a desired size, or feel free to just use scraps in the sizes that you already have.

1. Cut a center square, roughly 4" to 6" in size, from the black print fat quarter. Place the piece right side up in the center of a muslin square. Lay a scrap right side down on the center square as shown, making sure that the square below will be caught in the seam allowance. Sew with a ¼" seam allowance; press away from the center square. Before adding the next strip, trim the seam allowance to ¼" if needed to help reduce bulk. Lay another scrap right side down in the desired location and sew. Continue sewing and flipping until the entire square is filled, and then trim the block to 10½" x 10½". You will make 13 of these Crazy Quilt blocks.

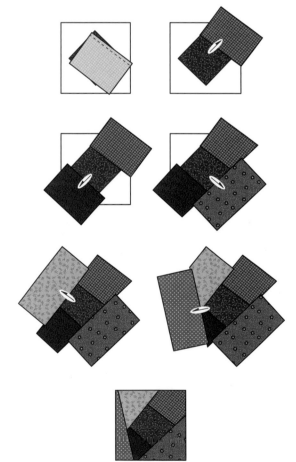

Make 13.

2. Referring to "Appliqué" on page 9, prepare the appliqué shapes from the patterns on page 118. Position the shapes on the black solid squares, referring to the photo on page 115 for placement. Machine appliqué using a blanket stitch with matching topstitching thread.

## Assembling the Quilt Top

1. Sew the blocks into five rows of five blocks each. Press all the seams toward the black blocks. Sew the rows together and press the seams in either direction. Proof the quilt-top center to 50½" x 50½".

2. Sew the 6½"-wide black solid strips together end to end and cut off four lengths at 50½". Prepare 48 "tongue" appliqué shapes and position them on the black strips, referring to the photo for placement. There are 12 tongues per side, about 2" to 2⅛" apart. Machine appliqué the shapes using a blanket stitch with black topstitching thread. Referring to "Adding the Borders" on page 8 as needed, sew two of the borders to the sides of the quilt top and press the seams away from the tongue border. Sew the 6½" black solid squares to the ends of the remaining strips and sew these to the top and bottom of the quilt, pressing the seams away from the border. Proof the quilt top to 62½" x 62½".

Make 4.

3. Sew the red print strips together end to end. Cut off two lengths at 62½" and sew them to the sides of the quilt top. Press the seams toward the red. Cut off two lengths at 72½" and sew these to the top and bottom of the quilt top; press.

4. Sew the black plaid strips together end to end. Cut off two lengths at 72½" and sew them to the sides of the quilt top. Press the seams toward the black. Cut off two lengths at 77" and sew these to the top and bottom of the quilt top; press. Proof the quilt top to 77" x 77".

5. Referring to "Half-Square-Triangle Units" on page 7, sew the 6¾" colored squares together to make 56 half-square-triangle units. Proof each unit to 6⅜" x 6⅜". Referring to "Folded-Corner Units" on page 7, sew the 2¼" black squares to two opposite corners of each unit as shown. Trim the seam to ¼" and press it toward the black.

Make 56.

6. Using the units from step 5, sew two rows of 13 units each. Proof the rows to a length of 77". Sew these to the sides of the quilt top and press the seams toward the black plaid. Sew the remaining units into two rows of 15 units each. Proof the rows to a length of 88¾". Sew these to the top and bottom of the quilt top; press.

7. From the remaining pieced black plaid strip, cut off two lengths at 88¾" and sew them to the sides of the quilt top, pressing the seams toward the black plaid. Cut off two lengths at 93¼" and sew these to the top and bottom of the quilt top; press.

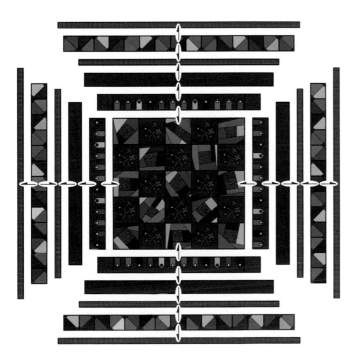

## Finishing

Refer to the quilt-finishing techniques on pages 12–13, if needed.

1. Piece the quilt backing so that it's approximately 4" wider and longer than the quilt top. Mark the quilt top if necessary. Layer the quilt top with batting and backing; baste the layers together. Hand or machine quilt as desired.

2. Trim the batting and backing even with the edges of the quilt top. Add a hanging sleeve if desired. Using the 2½"-wide green plaid strips, prepare the binding and sew it to the quilt.

### SIZE OPTION

For this quilt I chose to do a size option instead of a color option. I made seven of the Crazy Quilt blocks and cut several of them into halves and quarters. Then I used those pieces to set off the center appliqué blocks.

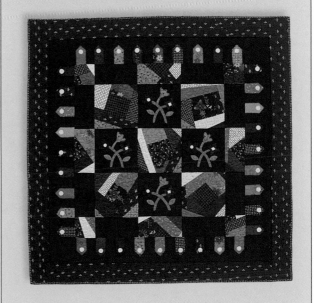

117

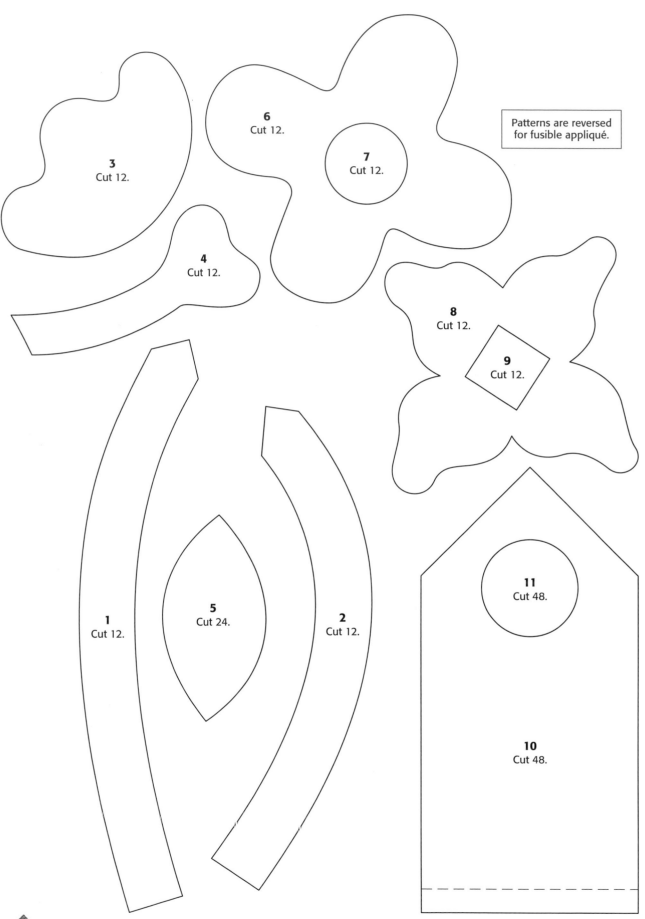

**3**
Cut 12.

**6**
Cut 12.

**7**
Cut 12.

Patterns are reversed
for fusible appliqué.

**4**
Cut 12.

**8**
Cut 12.

**9**
Cut 12.

**1**
Cut 12.

**5**
Cut 24.

**2**
Cut 12.

**11**
Cut 48.

**10**
Cut 48.

# Lone Star Sensation

**M**any quilters would love to make a lone star quilt, but have heard the horror stories of puckered middles and set-in pieces. The center of this quilt is made with half-square-triangle units. So, if you can make a simple half-square-triangle unit, you can make a lone star. The quilt has a dynamic layout and the large background squares beg for some fancy quilting.

## Materials

*Yardage is based on 42"-wide fabric. Materials are listed in order from the center out.*

¼ yard of red floral for star

¼ yard of cream print for star

⅓ yard of blue fabric for star

⅜ yard of black fabric for star

½ yard of green fabric for star

½ yard of yellow fabric for star

⅓ yard of brown fabric for star

¼ yard of red stripe for star

¼ yard of blue print for star

1⅔ yards of cream tonal for star background

1 yard of red paisley for first border

2⅝ yards of black floral for second border

3 yards *total* of assorted colored fabrics for outer border

⅞ yard of red fabric for binding

8½ yards of fabric for backing

100" x 100" piece of batting

## Cutting

**From the blue fabric, cut:**
1 strip, 3⅜" x 42"; crosscut into 12 squares, 3⅜" x 3⅜"

2 strips, 3" x 42"; crosscut into:
  12 squares, 3" x 3"
  4 pieces, 3" x 5½"

**From the red floral, cut:**
1 square, 5½" x 5½"

8 squares, 3" x 3"

**From the cream print, cut:**
4 squares, 5½" x 5½"

4 squares, 3" x 3"

**From the black fabric, cut:**
3 strips, 3⅜" x 42"; crosscut into 28 squares, 3⅜" x 3⅜"

Cut remainder of strip into 4 squares, 3" x 3"

**From the green fabric, cut:**
3 strips, 3⅜" x 42"; crosscut into 32 squares, 3⅜" x 3⅜"

1 strip, 3" x 42"; crosscut into 12 squares, 3" x 3"

Continued on page 121

Quilt size: 95½" x 95½"

**From the yellow fabric, cut:**

3 strips, 3⅜" x 42"; crosscut into 28 squares, 3⅜" x 3⅜"

1 strip, 3" x 42"; crosscut into 8 squares, 3" x 3"

**From the brown fabric, cut:**

2 strips, 3⅜" x 42"; crosscut into 20 squares, 3⅜" x 3⅜"

1 strip, 3" x 42"; crosscut into 8 squares, 3" x 3"

**From the red stripe, cut:**

2 strips, 3⅜" x 42"; crosscut into 12 squares, 3⅜" x 3⅜"

Cut remainder of strip into 8 squares, 3" x 3"

**From the blue print fabric, cut:**

1 strip, 3⅜" x 42"; crosscut into 4 squares, 3⅜" x 3⅜"

Cut remainder of strip into 8 squares, 3" x 3"

**From the cream tonal, cut:**

8 squares, 13⅜" x 13⅜"; cut each square once diagonally to yield 16 triangles

4 squares, 13" x 13"

**From the red paisley, cut:**

4 rectangles, 5½" x 23"

4 rectangles, 5½" x 18½"

**From the black floral, cut:**

4 rectangles, 8" x 30½"

4 rectangles, 8" x 25½"

4 rectangles, 8" x 13"

4 squares, 10½" x 10½"

**From the assorted colored fabrics, cut a *total* of:**

120 squares, 5½" x 5½"

**From the red binding fabric, cut:**

10 strips, 2½" x 42"

## Making the Blocks

1.  Referring to "Folded-Corner Units" on page 7, sew 3" blue squares and 3" red floral squares to the 5½" cream print squares as shown. Press the seams away from the cream print. Proof each unit to 5½" x 5½".

Make 4.

2.  Sew a 3" blue square to a 3" cream print square and press the seam toward the blue. Add a 3" x 5½" blue piece as shown and press toward the blue. Make four of these units and proof each unit to 5½" x 5½".

Make 4.

3.  Sew the units from steps 1 and 2 together with the 5½" red floral square as shown. Press the seams as directed and proof the Star block to 15½" x 15½".

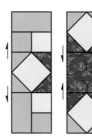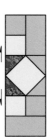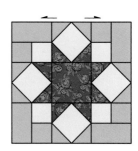

4.  Referring to "Half-Square-Triangle Units" on page 7, sew the 3⅜" squares together to make the following half-square-triangle unit combinations. Proof each unit to 3" x 3" and press the seams as directed by the arrows.

Make 24.    Make 32.    Make 32.

Make 24.    Make 16.    Make 8.

5. Border the Star block with the blue-and-black units and the four 3" black squares as shown. Next, border the block with the black-and-green units and four of the 3" green squares. Proof the block to 25½" x 25½".

6. Sew the remaining half-square-triangle units and 3" squares together as shown to make the star point sections. Trim each section, leaving a ¼" seam allowance past the points. Sew a 13⅜"

cream triangle to the section, and press toward the cream. Proof the squares to 13" x 13".

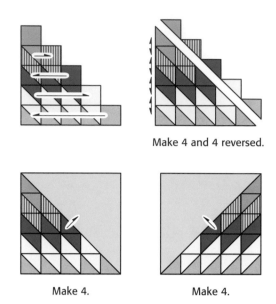

Make 4 and 4 reversed.

Make 4.          Make 4.

## Assembling the Quilt Top

1. Sew the squares from step 6 of "Making the Blocks" and the 13" cream squares to the Star block as shown. Press seams toward the cream pieces. Proof the quilt-top center to 50½" x 50½".

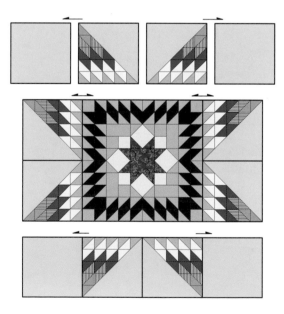

2. Sew an 18½"-long red paisley rectangle to a 25½"-long black floral rectangle as shown, pressing the seam toward the black. Align the 45° line of your ruler along the seam line and trim each unit. Add a 13⅜" cream triangle as shown and press toward the cream. Make two of these inner-border sections and two reversed. Sew the sections together in pairs as shown.

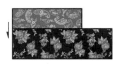 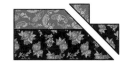

Make 2 and 2 reversed.

Make 2.

3. Repeat the previous step using the 23"-long red paisley rectangles and the 30½"-long black floral rectangles. Make two of these inner-border sections and two reversed, and then add an 8" x 13" black floral rectangle to the ends. Press toward the rectangles. Sew the sections together in pairs as shown.

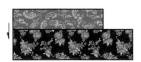 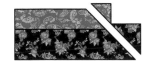

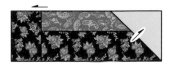

Make 2 and 2 reversed.

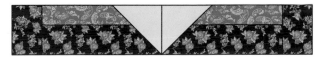

Make 2.

4. Referring to "Adding the Borders" on page 8 as needed, sew the inner-border rows to the quilt top, pressing the seams toward the inner border. Proof the quilt top to 75½" x 75½".

5. Sew the 5½" colored squares into four sections, each 2 squares wide by 15 squares long, as shown. Sew two sections to the quilt top, pressing the seams toward the colored squares. Add the 10½" black floral squares to the ends of the remaining sections, pressing the seams away from the black, and sew these to the quilt top. Press the seams toward the colored squares.

## Finishing

Refer to the quilt-finishing techniques on pages 12–13, if needed.

1. Piece the quilt backing so that it's approximately 4" wider and longer than the quilt top. Mark the quilt top if necessary. Layer the quilt top with batting and backing, and baste the layers together. Hand or machine quilt as desired.

2. Trim the batting and backing even with the edges of the quilt top. Add a hanging sleeve if desired. Using the 2½"-wide red strips, prepare the binding and sew it to the quilt.

# Nine Patch Posies

This quilt has a sweet elegance about it, inspired by a Nine Patch block. The cutting is simplified because you only have to cut one strip each from 10 different fabrics. These strips are then used for the Nine Patch blocks and the scrappy border.

## Materials

*Yardage is based on 42"-wide fabric.*

⅛ yard *each* of 9 different colored fabrics for Nine Patch blocks

1⅛ yards of green floral for outer border

1⅛ yards of cream fabric for background

⅝ yard of yellow plaid for alternate block and setting triangles

⅝ yard of light green fabric for pieced chain

½ yard of dark green fabric for pieced chain

⅛ yard of gold fabric for Nine Patch blocks

¾ yard of red check for binding

3½ yards of fabric for backing

61" x 61" piece of batting

## Cutting

**From the cream fabric, cut**
8 strips, 2¾" x 42"; crosscut into 36 pieces, 2¾" x 7¼"

5 strips, 2⅛" x 42"; crosscut into:
    8 pieces, 2⅛" x 14"
    8 pieces, 2⅛" x 7½"
2 strips, 1" x 42"; crosscut into 72 squares, 1" x 1"

**From *each* of the colored fabrics, cut:**
1 strip, 2¾" x 42"; crosscut into 4 squares, 2¾" x 2¾". Save remainder of each strip for inner border.

**From the dark green fabric, cut:**
5 strips, 2¾" x 42"; crosscut into 60 squares, 2¾" x 2¾"

4 squares, 2⅛" x 2⅛"

**From the gold fabric, cut:**
1 strip, 2¾" x 42"; crosscut into 9 squares, 2¾" x 2¾". Save remainder of strip for inner border.

**From the light green fabric, cut:**
6 strips, 2¾" x 42"; crosscut into 72 squares, 2¾" x 2¾"

**From the yellow plaid, cut:**
2 squares, 10¾" x 10¾"; cut each square twice diagonally to yield 8 side triangles

2 squares, 5⅝" x 5⅝"; cut each square once diagonally to yield 4 corner triangles

4 squares, 7¼" x 7¼"

**From the green floral, cut:**
6 strips, 6" x 42"

**From the red check, cut:**
2½"-wide bias strips to total 235" in length

Quilt size: 57⅜" x 57⅜"

## Making the Blocks

1. Referring to "Folded-Corner Units" on page 7, sew 1" cream 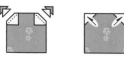 squares to 2¾" colored squares; press toward the cream.

Make 4 of each color (36 total).

2. Sew four matching units from step 1 together with four 2¾" dark green squares and one 2¾" gold square as shown. Press the seams away from the folded-corner units. Make nine different colored Nine Patch blocks and proof each block to 7¼" x 7¼".

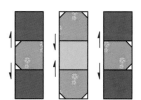

Make 1 of each color (9 total).

3. Using the folded-corner technique, sew the 2¾" light green squares to the 2¾" x 7¼" cream rectangles, pressing the seams toward the light green. Sew the remaining 2¾" dark green squares to each end of 12 of these units as shown, pressing the seam toward the dark green.

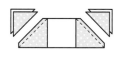

Make 36.

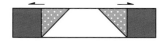

Make 12.

4. Sew each 2⅛" x 14" cream piece to the bottom of a 10¾" yellow plaid triangle as shown. Press the seams toward the yellow. Trim the cream pieces even with the sides of the triangles.

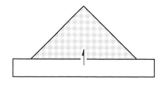 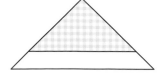

Make 8.

5. Sew a 2⅛" x 7½" cream piece to one side of a 5⅝" yellow plaid triangle as shown, pressing the seam toward the yellow. Sew a 2⅛" dark green square to the end of a 7½" cream piece, pressing the seam toward the green. Sew this strip to the other side of the triangle. Press this seam toward the yellow. Trim the cream pieces even with the bottom of the triangles.

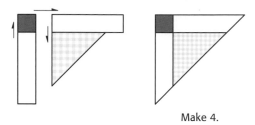

Make 4.

## Assembling the Quilt Top

1. Lay out the Nine Patch blocks, the 7¼" yellow plaid squares, both types of units from step 3 of "Making the Blocks," the side triangle units from step 4 of that section, and the corner triangle units from step 5 of that section as shown. Sew the pieces into rows, pressing all the seams as indicated. Sew the rows together, pressing the seams in either direction. Proof the quilt-top center to 41⅞" x 41⅞".

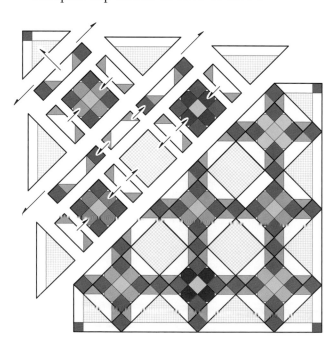

2. Referring to "Adding the Borders" on page 8 as needed, cut the remaining 2¾" colored strips into assorted lengths of 6" to 9" and sew these pieces together. Cut off two lengths at 41⅞" for the side inner borders and two lengths at 46⅜" for the top and bottom inner borders. Sew the side borders to the quilt top, pressing the seams toward the borders. Sew the top and bottom borders to the quilt top, pressing the seams toward the borders.

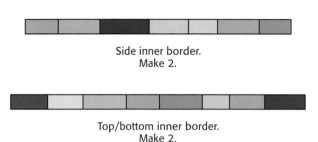

Side inner border.
Make 2.

Top/bottom inner border.
Make 2.

3. Sew the green floral strips together end to end. Cut off two lengths at 46⅜" for the side outer borders and two lengths at 57⅜" for the top and bottom outer borders. Sew the side borders to the quilt top, pressing the seams toward the green floral. Sew the top and bottom borders to the quilt top, pressing the seams toward the green floral.

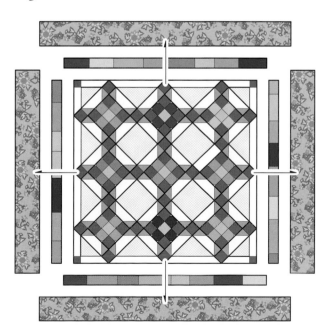

## Finishing

Refer to the quilt-finishing techniques on pages 12–13, if needed.

1. Piece the quilt backing so that it's approximately 4" wider and longer than the quilt top. Mark the quilt top if necessary. Layer the quilt top with batting and backing, and baste the layers together. Hand or machine quilt as desired.

2. Trim the batting and backing even with the edges of the quilt top. Add a hanging sleeve if desired. Using the 2½"-wide red check bias strips, prepare the binding and sew it to the quilt.

## COLOR OPTION

One of my fabric lines, Lakeside Cottage, inspired my color option for this quilt. I thought the pattern lent itself well to the colors, and the alternate squares and setting triangles were a perfect place to show off the large red floral.

# Meet the Author

My introduction to sewing and quilting began at an early age. My mother was always working in her sewing room and I was busy at her side, playing with the beautifully colored buttons and fabric swatches. By the age of five, I had my own sewing machine, a hand-me-down from my great-grandma Anka (after whom my business, Anka's Treasures, is named). By the age of 10 I was making mostly clothes, but I had put together several utilitarian quilts as well.

It wasn't until I was 19 that I really started quilting, and a whole new world opened up to me. At that time I was a freshman in college. I was taking my general courses, but the art classes I attended were my favorite. I felt that art might not be a marketable degree for me, though, and I was struggling to figure out my future. After a year of learning the basics of quilting, a small dream started, as I thought of the possibility of turning my favorite hobby into a job. Maybe I had found a way to make my art marketable after all.

I started small, working one job to pay for my schooling and another to fund my new business, all the while going to school full-time. One of the jobs included working at my local quilt shop. This is where I received my foundation in quiltmaking, from learning the basics to running a long-arm quilting machine.

This is also where I taught my first classes and learned that quilters are fun people to work with. Within a year or two, my business was able to support me and I quit my other jobs. Now, years later, I have published several books, numerous single patterns, and designs for quilting magazines and fabric lines.

I had my first inklings about designing when I discovered that I couldn't stick to a pattern. I always ended up making major changes. Then, in an astronomy class in college, we were given a tablet of graph paper for homework assignments. I discovered that most quilts are based on grids, and I spent many hours in that class doodling quilt blocks. By the end of that semester I had a whole tablet full of quilt pattern ideas, and I decided to try publishing a few. To this day, I still design with graph paper and colored pencils, rather than using a computer.

My husband, Joel, and I reside in Spicer, Minnesota. Two years ago we bought a fixer-upper on a lake there, and since then we have spent most of our free time remodeling the house. We have done much of the work ourselves, in the process learning more than we care to know about remodeling! My other hobbies include reading, knitting, kayaking, watching movies, and spending time with friends and family.